GE
Oil & Gas

VetcoGray subsea tree

For centuries, the spirit of innovation has run deep within the Florentine culture in both art and science.

The same goals of creativity and quality are the ones that we hold dear in every thing we do at GE Oil & Gas.

Claudi Santiago
President & CEO
GE's Oil & Gas Business

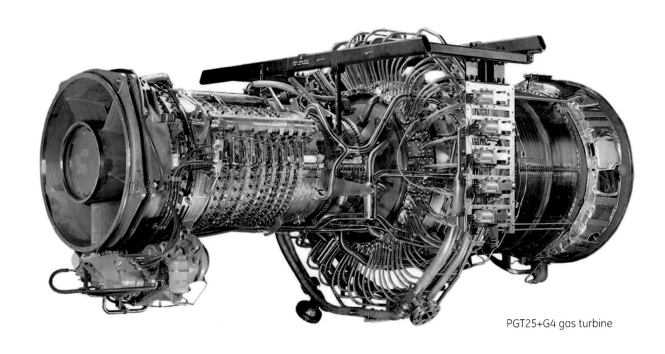

PGT25+G4 gas turbine

 imagination at work

WHITE STAR
PUBLISHERS

Tuscany
PLACES AND HISTORY

Texts
Costanza Poli

Design
Alberto Bertolazzi

Editing Supervision
Valeria Manferto De Fabianis

Translation
Neil Frazer Davenport

Art Director
Patrizia Balocco Lovisetti

1 The Calcio Storico is one of the oldest and most popular of the traditional Florentine festivals. The participants dress in Renaissance costumes and represent the four city quarters, San Giovanni, Santa Croce, Santa Maria Novella and Santo Spirito. Prior to the matches, drummers and flag twirlers stir up the crowd.

2-7 The volutes that enhance the facade of Santa Maria Novella in Florence were designed by Leon Battista Alberti: geomtrical patterns and floral decorations combine ine the soft classical motif that characterises the marble of one of the most beautiful Tuscan churches.

3-6 The golden yellow of the Sienese earth spreads over rolling hills punctuated by farmhouses. Like silent sentinels, the cypresses, unmistakable symbols of the Tuscan countryside, rise to mark a border or shade a winding road.

© 1996, 2000 White Star S.r.l.
Via C. Sassone, 22/24
13100 Vercelli, Italy.

ISBN 80-8095-550-0
2 3 4 5 6 05 04 03 02 01 00

Colour separations by Gai Scaligera, Verona. Printed in Italy by Grafedit, Bergamo.

CONTENTS

*T*uscany resists definition: in the global collective consciousness it is the Italian region par excellence and, even in its multifaceted diversity, it represents a cohesive historical, artistic and naturalistic entity that just happens to be situated right in the center of the peninsula. What follows are brief notes on the history and culture of the region. Rather than being comprehensive accounts, they are intended to act as spurs and invitations, to compel you to follow those twisting roads that wind their way among rolling hills, to lose yourselves in the labyrinthine streets and alleys of the medieval cities, to dream in front of a Tyrrhenian sunset as you stroll along the endless beaches of the Maremma or to contemplate the sea from the rocky shore of Elba. You are also invited to listen to the vernacular of the native Tuscans and to examine their faces for traces of their Etruscan or Roman forebears, to participate in the festivals and games that have long marked the return of spring, the veneration of saints and ancient battles and heroic enterprises. Visiting Tuscany is something of an obligatory rite of passage, and the region has something to offer to us all. Art here is no isolated monument, no single noble palace or solitary stela. It is something that permeates and is an indispensable, ineluctable aspect of everyday life. Here you can walk along roads worn by the feet of Giotto, Masaccio, Donatello and Michelangelo. Gaze at the banks of the Arno and you evoke memories of Dante, Boccaccio and Petrarch. The villas immersed in the countryside were the settings for the intellectual indulgences of Cosimo and Lorenzo dei Medici and the twilight years of Machiavelli. It was in the duomo at Pisa that Galileo Galilei had the intuition that changed the course of scientific thought. The Tuscan countryside has a perhaps less academic culture to relate, but one no less rich and varied. Over thousands of years agriculture has created a landscape so instantly recognizable that the term "Tuscan hills" has come to describe the exemplary molding of nature by the hand of humans. You can hardly visit the great cities of art and ignore the Sienese *Crete*, the *calanchi* of Pratomagno and the tufa hills of Grosseto. The Tuscan civilization has, moreover, always had a gently influential role, capable of showing the way, of developing an idea to its peak before withdrawing and leaving to others the task of exhausting its potential while it concentrates on inventing something new. It was thus in the fields of art and lit-

8 top Monteriggioni, the ancient Sienese outpost that was intended to halt the Florentine advance, is now a tranquil country town rising suddenly from the crown of a hill. The old town walls — reinforced by 14 square towers that were once much taller—conceal a fragment of medieval Tuscany that has remained virtually unchanged.

8-9 Montalcino, an ancient town perched atop a hill covered with vineyards and olive groves, looks out over the lush green Val d'Orcia. Today the name of this small town appears on the most sophisticated tables around the world thanks to Brunello di Montalcino, a fine wine that gives nothing away to its rivals from Bordeaux.

9 top The center of Lucignano, close to Monte San Savino, has retained the elliptical form dictated by the morphology of the hill on which it sits. The enchanting landscape of the Valdichiana extends in all directions.

erature in bygone centuries. Revolutions are not always the prerogatives of men of arms, at times all it takes is a man of creative genius to change the course of cultural history. In championing the Tuscan vernacular over Latin and the other idioms, Dante changed the history of the Italian language; turning his back on Byzantine iconography, Giotto introduced human passion to the representation of the divine. And, almost 500 years after the event, the scientific discoveries of Leonardo are still being studied. Today a similar process can be observed in terms of our perception of the quality of Tuscan life. Never before has a country house in Tuscany been so highly sought. The metropolises are being rejected as people seek out the peace and fresh greenery of the countryside or try to enter into the daily life of small towns that contain more works of art than the average European city. These immigrants are the last of a legion: ever since Roman times the dream of the serenity of Tuscan provincial life has captivated millions. The true Tuscans look on these would-be producers of olive oil and wine, barn restorers and holiday farm entrepreneurs with a hint of ironic sufferance. "Tuscanity" is not something that can be learned; it is a quality imbibed directly from mother's milk along with the aspirated Tuscan "c," a typical pronunciation of the region.

Uccellina National Park

Alpi Apuane
Carrara
Massa
Viareggio
Serchio
Lago di Massaciuccoli
Lucca
Pisa
Arno
Ligurian Sea

Appennino Tosco-Emiliano

Pistoia
Prato
Montecatini Terme
Florence
Scandicci
Empoli
San Miniato
Livorno
San Gimignano
Arezzo
Volterra
Cecina
Siena
Cortona
Isola di Gorgona
Cecina
Cecina

Montepulciano
Civitella
Montalcino
Chianciano Terme

Isola di Capraia
Follonica
Piombino
Portoferraio
Gulf of Follonica
Bruna
Ombrone
Isola d'Elba
Porto Azzurro
Grosseto

Tuscan
Archipelago
Monti dell'Uccellina
Albegna
Lago di Orbetello
Isola di Pianosa
Orbetello
Porto Santo Stefano
Port'Ercole
Isola di Montecristo
Isola del Giglio
Monte Argentario

Tyrrhenian Sea
Isola di Giannutri

The Vernaccia vinyards with
San Gimignano in the background.

The Sienese hills.

The Ponte Vecchio, Florence.

Piazza dei Miracoli at Pisa.

The Duomo of Siena

To the Romans they were known as the *Tusci* or the *Etruschi* while to the Greeks they were the *Tyrrhenians*: what is clear is that the Etruscans are the ancestors of the modern Tuscans, even though only a few of the most important centers of their ancient civilization lay within the current boundaries of the region. The original Etruria comprised the area between the Arno and the Tevere rivers and thus included broad sweeps of both Umbria and Lazio, while excluding the modern-day Tuscan provinces of Massa Carrara and Lucca, which were then Ligurian territory. One theory regarding the origin of the Etruscan people goes back to Herodotus and the state of Lydia from where they fled shortly after the Trojan War. Another has the Etruscans descending from Tyrrhenian-Pelasgian pirates, while Latin historian Livy claimed that they had arrived from regions beyond the Alps. More recent theses claim that the Etruscans were the result of a fusion between the native people and immigrants from the East. What is of most interest is the cultural supremacy achieved by the Etruscans. They created a sophisticated civilization that reached its peak in the 7th century BC, when the power and wealth of the Etruscan aristocracy allowed the importation of products in gold, silver, ivory and bronze from the East, from Egypt

and from Greece. The gradual decline of this civilization—partly caused by military defeats—and the final coup de grâce provided by the rise of Rome destroyed a society that today we know of only through indirect sources, archaeological finds and historical accounts. The Etruscan cities, such as Vetulonia, Populonia, Volterra and Arezzo to name but four, were city-states comparable to the Greek polis and dominated the surrounding lands with alliances, a fragmentation that made a major contribution to their eventual demise. The triumph of Rome and the reduction of Etruria to the status of a province were confirmed with the construction of two consular roads. The Via Aurelia ran along the coast while the interior was served by the Via Cassia that linked Bolsena, Chiusi and Arezzo. The Apennines and the Arno River were the natural barriers to the two arteries that terminated at Luni and Fiesole. A third road, the Clodia, entered into the heart of Etruria and joined up with the Via Aurelia. These routes are still valid and can be found unchanged as parts of the current Tuscan road network. Well off these tracks the Romans established military bases that became great cities of art and arms: Lucca, Pistoia, Florence and Pisa all conserve the structure of the Roman *castrum*, with its *cardo* and *decumano*.

20-21 The tomb of Ildebrand in the Etruscan necropolis at Sovana, one of the tufa towns in the province of Grosseto. This is one of the best preserved tombs in an area in which there are numerous traces of the settlements of the ancient civilization.

21 top The grandiose Roman theater at Volterra dates back to imperial times. Parts of the stage, the cavea and the portico remain, the latter containing a thermal bath. Among the wealth of Etruscan remains in the area is Velathri, the city of alabaster.

21 top right The Arco Gate at Volterra is inserted into the remains of massive walls and faces out over the valley.

21 bottom right The Tomb of the Pilgrim in the Etruscan necropolis carved into the tufa at Chiusi contains sarcophagi and funerary urns. It is one of the most famous burial sites, along with the Scimmia and Colle tombs. The search for the legendary Porsenna tomb described by the ancient writers has proven fruitless.

Following the fall of the Roman Empire in the West, the invasions by Theodoric and the wars between the Ostrogoths and the Byzantines weakened the Tuscia region and in the middle of the 6th century the Longobards were able to walk in unopposed. It was however, this conquest that marked the beginning of the rebirth of the region. The protracted Longobard dominion (until 774) saw, above all, a growth in the importance of Lucca. Chosen as a ducal fiefdom, the city was linked to the Padana plain via the Cisa Pass. At the same the influence of Pisa also expanded and the city became a major trading power from its Tyrrhenian base. The accession to power of Charlemagne marked the onset of an administrative "revolution" and confirmed the influence of the bishops who wielded both spiritual and secular power. Under the Carolingians the number of castles devoted to the defense of the region increased, and after the year 1000 the region witnessed a period of growth. The first effect of this turn of events was the building of new churches. With the help of the faithful, it was the local aristocrats who promoted this religious building spree: there began a noble race to erect the largest abbey, the most popular convent, the most venerated chapel. Then there were the *pievi*, a kind of country parish directly dependent on

the bishoprics; the *pievi* enjoyed great privileges in the 11th century. Here the faithful were baptised and buried and also saw justice administered. Even though they were situated outside the inhabited centers, the *pievi* immediately became poles of attraction. While many of the ancient coastal towns such as Luni, were abandoned, Pisa went from strength to strength as via its port it maintained contacts with Corsica, Sardinia and the coast of North Africa, laying the basis for the Marine Republic. Feudal Tuscany was a conglomerate of potentates, frequently led by bishops with all the power of earls, making it more of a mosaic than a united region. It was this structure that allowed the communes to develop, and then demand political and cultural autonomy. In the meantime another element, religion, began to change the face of the region. The foundation of the Orders of the Camoldolesi and the Vallombrosani were to have great influence over Tuscan life and its history. At the center of these events were the great cities that began their struggle for preeminence, prior to demolishing the remaining traces of the Tuscan marquisate. Feudalism continued to exist only in the poorest areas such as the Lunigiana, the Casentino, the Val Tiberina and part of the Maremma; the future of Tuscany lay with the city-states.

22 The Basilica di San Francesco at Assisi was undoubtedly built to the greater glory of the saint, but it is also true that the work of Giotto is so extensive and successful here that the building might well have been dedicated at least in part to the artist. This illustration shows a scene from the episode in which St. Francis drives the demons from Arezzo. Given the realism employed by the artist, it is reasonable to suppose that this is a reliable record of the city in the 14th century.

23 top A work by Domenico Lenzi, known as il Biadaiolo, conserved in the Laurenziana Library in Florence, reveals the wealthy and industrious appearance of the 14th-century city in which every inhabitant, men women and priests, had clearly defined roles.

23 bottom In the sacristy of San Miniato al Monte in Florence there is a fresco cycle by Spinello Aretino and his pupils dedicated, above all, to the figure of San Benedetto. In this scene the saint recognizes King Totila.

24 top left The battle of Montaperti—illustrated by Giovanni di Ventura in a codex in the City Library at Siena—took place on the 4th September 1260, and was fought between the Guelphs of Florence and the Ghibellines of Siena. The battle, recorded by Dante in the 10th and 32nd cantos of his Inferno, was won by the Ghibellines, who consigned the Guelphs to exile.

24 top right The gold florin, minted for the first time in Florence in 1252, was the symbol of the economic primacy of Florence throughout Tuscany and of its international prestige.

The Tuscan cities were free of, or at least attempted to maintain their autonomy from, the authority of the papacy and the empire, although they did align themselves with one or the other. This situation represented the birth of the communes, and Florence, Pisa, Siena, Lucca and Arezzo competed among themselves, gradually eliminating the feudal territories. The "Queen" of the 13th century was Pisa. The city participated in the Crusades, mounted a raid against the Moors in the Balearics and attempted to expand, although defeat at Meloria (1284) against the Genoans marked the beginning of its decline. At the same time began the irresistible rise of Florence that even in the early years of the century had begun to undermine the economic power of Siena, which until that moment had been the "bank" of the Holy See. The conflict between the Guelphs and the Ghibellines, the most significant event in Tuscany in the 13th century, is proof that the struggle for power in the region was between two well-defined social strata. The great noble families, stripped of their feudal rights, were unwilling to accept the rise of their rivals, the mercantile class, the bourgeoisie, who were unwilling to accept the interference of the empire in their affairs and development. The Guelphs were to prevail, following the Ghibellines' brief victory at Montaperti in 1260. Within this political climate the dominion of Florence also extended throughout much of the region. In the 14th century the city conquered, with arms or money, Arezzo, Prato and shortly afterwards Pisa, Cortona and Livorno. Wealthy in terms of gold and prestige— the gold *fiorino*, first minted in 1252, was already the dominant coin—Florence was searching for a leader who would put an end to the oligarchic government. She found this leader first in the charismatic figure of Cosimo dei Medici, also known as Cosimo the Elder, and then in Lorenzo il Magnifico.

24-25 Following his victory over Castruccio Castracani, the Sienese authorities commissioned Simone Martini, the painter of the Maestà *in the Palazzo Pubblico, to celebrate the virtues of Guidoriccio da Fogliano in a grandiose work of art. The hero of Monte Massi is portrayed alone between two conquered castles. Behind lies his camp, before him lies his triumph.*

25 The Guelph (bottom) and Gibelline (top) seals. The two factions fought for power in Italy between the 13th nd the 14th centuries, the former as supporters of the papacy, the latter in favor of the Holy Roman Empire. In reality, behind the formal positions lay intense personal rivalries between the two noble families.

26 top The Codice Miniato of 1472, conserved in the State Archive at Siena, shows that trade, like all other activities, was controlled by precise norms. Good government was a blend of Liberalism and strict formal control.

26 bottom The Salone dei Cinquecento in the Palazzo Vecchio in Florence was built on the orders of Savonarola and was intended to house 500 councillors following the departure of the Medici. However, it was a Medici, Cosimo I, who commissioned Giorgio Vasari to extend the hall and decorate it with fresco panels celebrating the city. In this scene Pisa is being attacked by the Florentine troops.

26-27 The Sienese school of the 14th century boasted a long series of talented followers of Simone Martini and the Lorenzetti brothers: Bartolo di Fredi, in this Adoration of the Magi, now in the Pinacoteca Nazionale in Siena, shows a realistic glimpse of his city at the height of its glory.

27 top This work by Pontormo, now in the Uffizi, shows an idealized portrait of Cosimo the Elder, an extremely wealthy businessman who became the arbiter of Florentine political life, exercising a de facto hegemony for 30 years and establishing the Medici dynasty.

27 bottom This work, in the Museo degli Argenti in Florence, represents the port of Livorno in 1560. The silting up of the port of Pisa in the 16th century favored the development of Livorno, which became the most important of the Medici dominions. Work on the port continued up until the beginning of the 17th century.

28 top
The martyrdom
of Girolamo
Savonarola.
His passionate
accusations of
corruption among the
clergy and politicians
and his fervent

demands for reform
and democracy led to
his excommunication
by Pope Alexander
VI in 1497. Arrested
and found guilty, he
was first hanged and
then his body was set
on fire.

28-29 Vincenzo
Rustici, the
Presentazione delle
Contrade in the
Piazza del Campo
and the Gioco con
Tori in Piazza del
Campo. The two
works show how deeply

sport is embedded in
the Sienese spirit. In
the shadow of the
Mangia Tower, in the
terracotta bowl of the
campo, every event
was—and still is—an
opportunity for
competition.

*L*orenzo il Magnifico was the latter, an astute and brilliant politician, the de facto lord of the city, who unified the Florentine dominions, providing them with a solid structure capable of resisting external influence. Subsequent events, with the government of Florence disputed between the promoters of the republican oligarchy and the Medici family, concluded with the rise to power of the first Grand Duke of Tuscany, Cosimo I, in 1537. The passage from the era of the communes to the authority of a recognized lord had been completed and for almost 40 years the activities of Cosimo I were inseparable from the development of Tuscany itself, as he governed the region with a sure and enthusiastic hand. His work contributed to the political unity of the area and the reforms set underway created an absolute state, but he was also responsible for streamlining the administrative structures and attempting to establish the equality of all Tuscan citizens before the law.

A personality as strong as that of Cosimo I inevitably overshadows those of his successors. Francesco Maria is of note above all for his interest in court life and his policy of strict observance of the pro-Spanish line. His brother Ferdinand, on the other hand was a cardinal who returned to secular life to occupy himself with the affairs of the state and preferred to seek the support of the French. He is best remembered for his work at Livorno and his attempts to reclaim certain marshy areas of the Grand Duchy. The Medici family's attempts to free themselves of the Spanish hegemony continued under Cosimo II, while under Ferdinand II the region was struck by two great disasters, famine due to poor harvests and plague, as well as the unstoppable decline of its economic position. At this time only Livorno, with its grandiose, open port, escaped the effects of the general recession. The demise of the Medici dynasty was hastened by this climate of crisis and corruption, and on the death of Gian Gastone in 1737, the Grand Duchy eventually passed into the hands of the Bourbon of Spain and then into the hands of the House of Lorraine. This marked the end of the story of the Medici family, its period of great splendor followed by a long, tormented decline.

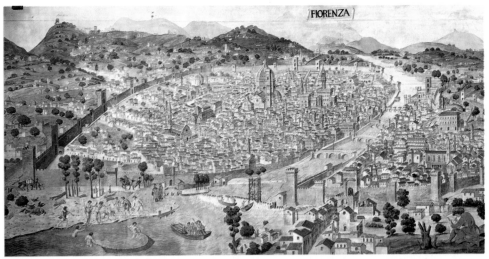

30-31 Lorenzo il Magnifico portrayed among artists in a work by Ottavio Vannini. Lorenzo's fame as a patron of the arts was well deserved. Among his interests, in addition to literature, were the collection of antiquities and books, music and philosophy. Moreover, he promoted culture in the broadest sense by instituting the Studio Generale of Pisa.

31 top Florence at the end of the 15th century, reconstructed in a 19th-century painting conserved in the Topographical Museum. The city appears as a hive of activity and well-being surrounded by imposing walls.

32-33 The ideal of courtly love is well represented by Benozzo Gozzoli. In his work, Viaggio dei Magi, in the Palazzo Medici-Riccardi in Florence, he depicted Lorenzo dei Medici in the caravan of the three kings in all his usual magnificence, together with his family and trusted archers.

T he accession to the throne of Peter Leopold of Lorraine in 1765 marked the beginning of the rebirth of the territory. The young grand duke—he was just eighteen years old—looked to the grandiose figure of Cosimo for inspiration and was aided by illustrious collaborators, such as Pompeo Neri, Angelo Tavanti and Francesco Maria Gianni, supporters of a liberal economic policy. With the land reclamation in the Maremma, the Val de Chiana and around Pisa—via the excavation of canals, the reconstruction of the port of Castiglione della Pescaia and benefits conceded to those willing to settle in these areas—the improvements in the communications network with new routes through the Apennines being opened up, the administrative and judiciary reforms and the abolition of torture and the death penalty, over a period of 25 years Peter Leopold tried to drag Tuscany into the modern age. Among his initiatives was the renewal of the agricultural system with the auctioning of the Medici possessions, a reform that transformed Tuscany into a region of small landowners. Then there was the abolition of the art and craft corporations and an unsuccessful attempt to revive the manufacturing industry. This ambitious reforming program was crowned by a written constitution drawn up by Francesco Maria Gianni.

34 top Maria Luisa Bourbon, the wife of Charles IV of Spain, married Ludovico di Bourbon-Parma in 1795, and with him ascended to the throne of Etruria. Following the Napoleonic events and the Congress of Vienna, she was assigned the Duchy of Lucca, which she led with great energy.

34 bottom Francis I of the Holy Roman Empire; Francis Stephen, the Duke of Lorraine; Francis II, the Grand Duke of Tuscany and Duke of Parma and Piacenza, all legitimate titles for the son of the Duke of Lorraine. Leopold, in spite of being formally at the head of the Grand Duchy of Tuscany, never lived in Florence and was represented by a regency council.

34-35 Peter Leopold of Hapsburg-Lorraine, the Grand Duke of Tuscany from 1765 to 1790—portrayed here in a family group by Wilhelm Berczy—was a great reformer with a passion for civil and economic liberty, good and honest administration and local self-government. His masterpiece was a new penal code inspired by Beccaria that abolished torture and capital punishment.

35 top Charles VIII of France entered Florence in 1494 through the Porta San Frediano and was welcomed by the populace who had rebelled against the power of the Medici. In reality, Charles was only passing through Florence on his way to the Kingdom of Naples and, in 1512 the Florentine Medici family regained control of the city.

36 This watercolor by Terrani depicts a ball at Pisa held in honor of Peter Leopold I. Between 1778 and 1782 the grand duke promoted the development of a project for a political constitution based on electoral representation.
It was never put into practice as the grand duke was called to the Imperial throne at Vienna.

36-37 A palio in Siena dedicated to Francis II and Maria Theresa, the daughter of Charles IV. Having ascended to the throne following the extinction of the Medici line, and being but a mediocre ruler, Francis was to be remembered in Tuscany above all as the father of Peter Leopold.

38 top A painting by
Emilio Burci dated
1868 shows the banks
of the Arno, the Ponte
alle Grazie and, to
the top right, San
Miniato al Monte.
The Ponte alle Grazie
was destroyed by the
Germans during the
Second World War
after having resisted
flooding for centuries.
It was subsequently
replaced by a modern
construction.

38-39 Piazza Santa
Croce, bordered by the
basilica and the
palazzi, has ever since
the Middle Ages been
the favorite site for
celebrations, games
and tournaments.
This picture by
Giovanni Signorini
shows the Florentine
carnival.

When Peter Leopold acceded to the imperial throne, he was succeeded by Ferdinand III. His long and troubled reign was marked by the Napoleonic period. During the French Revolution Tuscany maintained a neutral position in spite of the presence of a British fleet in the Tyrrhenian Sea and diplomatic pressure to join the anti-revolution coalition. In 1799 the Duchy of Lucca was invaded by the French troops: with the aristocratic republic declared void, a provisional government took power. The same happened in Florence following the departure of Ferdinand. This was a dark age for Tuscany, with popular uprisings in support of the restoration while in Siena there were even bonfires lit to burn the Jacobin followers. The Sanfedista "revolt" brought the grand duke back to the throne and shortly afterwards the Austrian troops put an end to the disorders. However, following the Treaty of Lunéville, the Grand Duchy was once again taken out of the hands of the House of Lorraine and the Bourbons of Parma were installed in Florence. Napoleon had changed the structure of the newborn Kingdom of Etruria with reforms and innovations brought in from France. The restoration had the effect of sweeping away the ephemeral dominion of Bonaparte and in 1815 the Congress of Vienna established the status of the Grand Duchy of Tuscany. Ferdinand III returned to the throne; his blood ties with the house of Austria determined his foreign policy, but in domestic terms he managed to create conditions of peace and tranquility with a degree of harmony. It was in this period that two of the most important institutions in Italian intellectual life were created, the Gabinetto Viessieux as well as the Accademia Georgofili, which dealt with the technical progress and development of the region. Leopold II, the grand duke from 1824, was a mild,

39 *Piazza della Signoria in a 19th-century painting: the ladies in crinolines and the gentlemen in top hats have been replaced by the millions of tourists who swarm here to visit Florence, regarded as the shapely daughter of Rome.*

tolerant sovereign who made Tuscany a secure asylum for exiled patriots, thus defusing attempts at internal rebellion. He was also responsible for the revival of the land reclamation schemes, the reopening of the iron ore mine on Elba and, in 1847, for the annexation of the Duchy of Lucca. Freedom of the press and an official statute, as well as Tuscany's participation in the wars of independence, opened up the borders of the Grand Duchy, but the activities of extremist groups and the revolt at

40-41 *The Second World War had a devastating effect on Florence: all the bridges over the Arno were destroyed with the exception of the Ponte Vecchio, and as they retreated the Nazi troops also demolished two broad areas on either side of the river.*
The reconstruction of the city set underway

immediately was based on a town plan that made provisions for great changes to the road network, but it did not have the desired effect.

Livorno led to Leopold's exile at Gaeta and shattered the good relations established between the grand duke—who abandoned Tuscany in 1859—and his subjects. The provisional government and the plebiscite of 1860 marked the region's absorption into the Kingdom of Sardinia. The new king entered Florence and between 1865 and 1870 the city was the capital of the Kingdom of Italy.

In conclusion, a few words on the immense damage in terms of human life and works of art suffered by Tuscany and Florence in particular during the Second World War. On the night of August 3, 1944, all the bridges over the Arno with the exception of the Ponte Vecchio were destroyed. That one remaining link was, however, blocked by the rubble from the demolition of the surrounding medieval quarters, mined by the Germans during their retreat. Natural disasters led to the Arno bursting its banks in 1966, and in 1993 a terrorist bomb caused the deaths of innocent victims, destroyed the home of the Accademia dei Georgofili and badly damaged the Uffizi galleries.

41

LANDSCAPES

Tuscany is the region that, at least in terms of landscape, best represents Italy in its entirety, a region in which variety is united in a harmonious whole. It is rather a region of transition between the North and the South, but not for this one of mediation. It is rather a region that has always had its own identity; so much so that the phrase "Tuscan landscape" is used throughout the world to describe any place where, by some happy coincidence, there are rolling hills, knolls and valleys covered in lush greenery and possibly vineyards or olive groves. The hills that are central to the Tuscan landscape are perhaps, together with the coast, the area that has been most affected by the intervention of humans over the course of the centuries. Quite remarkably these interventions have actually "improved" on what could already have been described as perfection. Agriculture has found a place within the great natural scheme of things, exploiting every opportunity without altering the underlying structure. Even the earth-colored rural houses and the sinuous roads lined with cypresses are integral parts of the harmonious whole. Just as important in the topography of central Tuscany are the great villas. It would be impossible to compile here even a partial list of the noble estates that punctuate the countryside. The villas were usually built as a *buen retiro*, a place in which to escape from the city and political cares. But they were also symbols of

42 *In the Chianti region the vineyards are the dominant feature of the landscape, adapting themselves to the terrain and occasionally allowing space for the residences of the landowners—top, a villa at Carmignano—or the rustic houses of the farmers.*

43 *The landscape of the Val d'Elsa cloaked in morning mist, as seen from the towers of San Gimignano: thus must have appeared the Tuscan countryside centuries ago.*

the interest their owners nurtured in proper management of their agricultural land. The most well-known and celebrated area of Tuscany is probably the Chianti region set between the Arno and Ombrone rivers: a fairly small area but one that has become universally famous thanks to its wine. The vineyards of the Chianti—Sangiovese, Canaiolo nero, Malvasia and Trebbiano bianco grapes are combined to produce a ruby

44 High on a tufa upland, the village of Sorano is a mosaic of tall houses locked into one another in the typical medieval pattern. The 16th-century fortress is said to have been designed by Antonio Maria Lari.

red masterpiece—follow the contours of the hillsides. The Etruscans were the first people to cultivate vines in the area, thus initiating that morphological evolution that characterizes the Chianti hills. Subsequently, the monasteries continued their work, and the wealth of the area gave rise to that immense architectural patrimony that interrupts the regular agricultural patterns: blessed with the warm tones of the local stone, it includes farmhouses and castles, *pievi* and minute towns in which time appears to have stood still. History and geography have put the Chianti region between Florence and Siena, and art has placed a fundamental role in its definition. A town such as Certaldo, dominated by the red of the bricks, with its crenellated towers, its walls and silent alleys, could be taken as a paradigm of the towns of the region as a whole. So could San Gimignano, where architecture and nature are fused. A day in San Gimignano is probably one of the most emotional experiences a traveler could hope for: the village grew up on the Via Francigena, the most important medieval road. Wealthy thanks to trading along the route, San Gimignano eventually boasted 65 towers; just eight remain to remind us of past glories. But set out below those eight towers are the walls

45 top At Pitigliano the tufa is indistinguishable from the houses, a natural bastion that in the past made a significant contribution to the defense of the town. Having passed to the Orsini family, Pitigliano was classified as a city and enjoyed the prestige of bishopric. It was the powerful Tuscan family who equipped the town with fortifications designed by Antonio da Sangallo.

46 top *The gorges of the Balze around Volterra have over the course of the centuries swallowed necropoli, Etruscan walls and country houses. But they have also put a brake on the urban expansion of the town, thus preserving its medieval structure.*

46 center
The calanchi *reveal the red earth of the Sienese* Crete, *in the surroundings of Monte Oliveto.*

46 bottom *Volterra, from its high spur of rock, dominates the surrounding countryside and the Balze (cliffs), as dramatic to the eye as they are dangerous to nearby buildings.*

46-47 *Volterra was one of the 12 Etruscan Lucumonie, and its importance is revealed by the dimensions of the ancient walls of which long stretches survive. Today the city lives principally on tourism and the working of alabaster.*

of the town, the Colle-giata di Santa Maria Assunta, the Piazza della Cisterna and great paintings and sculpture: frescoes by Taddeo di Bartolo, Benozzo Gozzoli and Barna da Siena, and two wooden statues by Jacopo della Quercia. In the Santa Fina Chapel there are veritable jewels of the art of Domenico Ghirlandaio and Benedetto da Maiano, enclosed in one of the most beautiful and representative examples of Tuscan Romanesque architecture. A perfect, self-contained miniature world that has remained intact since the 14th century. Not far away lies the province of Volterra, an area of unusual geological features set between the coastal region of Livorno and the Val d'Elsa. The provincial capital was one of the 12 Etruscan *lucumonie*—its importance is demonstrated by the size of the city walls dating from the 4th century BC. The city now lives on tourism and the working of the alabaster extracted

from the nearby quarries. In spite of its relative affluence, Volterra is faced by the threat of destruction: the *Balze*, or cliffs, on which it is built are subject to sudden subsidence that over the course of the centuries has swallowed necropoli and Etruscan remains and now endangers buildings such as the Badia Camoldese of San Giusto and San Clemente. The city manages to live with this threat, and it is perhaps its very precariousness that has saved it from speculation and rampant modernisation. Proceeding along the Via Francigena beyond Siena, one encounters another geological phenomenon, the Sienese *Crete*. These are the bleakest and most barren hills of the Valdelsa; they are known as the "Tuscan Desert" due to the yellow, gray, ocher and red coloring of the bare hilltops eroded by water that in places has excavated deep gorges. Among the fields of corn there are monuments of

48 left Early summer is a glorious season on the Sienese hills. The fields of grain are dotted with flowers and the crop is ripening, almost ready for the harvest and the beginning of a new cycle.

48 top and 48-49 The Sienese hills are proof that humankind can work in harmony with an extraordinarily beautiful landscape. One of the symbols of the Tuscan countryside are the cypresses that in addition to being decorative offer points of reference and provide particularly fine timber.

49 Isolated settlements, with houses set in the farmland, are a typical feature of the Sienese countryside. In this case it is likely to be the residence of a wealthy family as the estate has its own chapel.

incomparable beauty. Here medieval piety was responsible for the construction of some of most famous abbeys in Tuscany, including Monte Oliveto Maggiore immersed in a forest of holm oaks and cypresses and as robust as a fortress but softened by the frescoes of Luca Signorelli and Sodoma—splendor that contrasts with the highly evocative remains of the abbey of San Galgano, isolated in the valley of the Merse. Begun in the Gothic style in the 13th century, the abbey was a center of faith and culture for 200 years. Its decline set in early, however, and culminated with the collapse of its bell tower onto the roof. Abandoned and stripped of its precious fittings, today the church lies in ruins; what little remains is lovingly tended by a small community of nuns. A small community of French monks takes care of Sant'Antimo, the beautiful abbey in delicate roseate travertine and onyx close to Montalcino in the Val d'Orcia: attending the Sunday Mass and hearing the Gregorian chants that echo in the silence of the valley is a mystical experience. The medieval town of Montalcino is another center of the noble art of wine-making: it is here that the famous Brunello is produced, and each cellar claims to give life to the most precious bottles.

50 top left
In Tuscany the
location of rural
buildings depends on
two factors: on the
one hand the need for
the farmer and his
family to live close to
their land, and on
the other the search
for a pleasant, open
site, perhaps adorned
with cypresses.

50 center left A flock
of sheep. The animals
are mainly reared by
Sardinian shepherds,
and the mild or
mature Sienese
pecorino cheese is one
of Tuscany's
gastronomic treats.

50 bottom left The
Romanesque pieve of
Artimino on the
slopes of Mount
Albano, seen though
an olive grove.

The beauty of the landscape and the stone-built villages of San Quirico, Bagni Visconti —with its great water-filled main square—and, above all Pienza, the ideal city designed by Rossellino for Pope Pius II, is sufficient in itself to satisfy the more abstemious visitors. Not faraway another architectural jewel, Montepulciano, lies between the Val d'Orcia and the Valdichiana. An aristocratic town, favored by its geographical position, Montepulciano is a compact summary of Tuscan art, influenced by both Florence and Siena. The high point is perhaps the pilgrimage church of the Madonna of San Biagio designed by Antonio Sangallo the Elder. Set outside the town, surrounded by cypresses, it is one of the most successful examples of the integration of sublime art and nature.

Yet another different landscape greets those who turn toward Monte Amiata, the gateway to the Maremma. The mountain was actually once an active volcano and seems almost out of place among the hills of the region. An almost perfect cone covered with woodland, for many years it was an important source of mercury. The surrounding villages contain memorials to Davide Lazzaretti, the "Christ of the Amiata," who was shot in 1878. You can climb

50 right Crop
diversification is a
feature of the Sienese
countryside and
creates, especially in
the summer,
chromatic effects
worthy of a great
artist.

51 It is simply an
anonymous road in
the vicinity of
Monticchiello in Val
d'Orcia, and yet the
colors, the cypresses
and the softness of the
hills make it a
natural masterpiece.

52 top The influence of both Florence and Rome made Montepulciano a city rich in Renaissance palazzi, thanks in part to the special status it was given by the Medici.

In this photo of the Palazzo Comunale, designed by Michelozzo in the 14th century, you can clearly see traces of the Palazzo della Signoria in Florence.

52-53 Set in the center of the mining area of the Grosseto Maremma, Massa Marittima features a medieval nucleus that converges on the irregular piazza in front of the Duomo, the Palazzo Pretorio and the Palazzo Comunale. The photo on the left shows the campanile of the Duomo.

53 top Still enclosed within its ancient walls, Cortona has preserved its Etruscan-Roman plan over which the medieval town developed.

53 bottom Colle Val d'Elsa is composed of two separate parts: Colle Alta, the higher town, has conserved its medieval appearance with important monumental buildings and the 13th-century city walls. Arnolfo di Cambio, famous sculptor and architect, is said to have been born in one of the tower houses.

Mount Labbro on foot to pay homage at the great cross erected in his honor; for your efforts you are rewarded with a 360-degree panoramic view across to the tufa towns of Sorano, Sovana and Pitigliano. The Maremma here is still green and rich in water and in the various villages Etruscan memories blend with those of noble families: the Orsini, local lords since 1503, left their mark and alongside the tufa houses rise imposing castles and massive fortifications. Not faraway, Saturnia, with its sulphurous spa waters and Etruscan connections, has become a sophisticated tourist destination set in an undulating landscape that becomes increasingly flat and barren. The classic Maremma ("wild country, an obscure route exposed the threat of bandits and thieves" wrote Giovanni Sercambi in the early 15th century) was for centuries one of the unhappiest areas of Tuscany, damned by malaria, enemy raids and chronic poverty. Paradoxically, in the Etruscan and Roman eras this was a flourishing region producing wine and olive oil, and the remains of the noble villas reveal their owners' devotion to their land. The abandonment and swamping of the coasts brought disease and misery, a situation that only began to change with the intervention of Peter Leopold in the second half of the 16th and beginning of the 17th century. Grosseto, the provincial capital, expanded at the expense of the ancient Roselle and is today a large town clustered around its substantial walls. The

Maremma has now been dominated by man: fields of grain, olive groves and herds of cattle guided by the *butteri*, the Tuscan cowboys who could have taught a thing or two even to Buffalo Bill. Descending toward the Tyrrhenian Sea, the Mediterranean maquis vegetation begins to dominate. The Parco dell'Uccellina, a dense green oasis, was founded in 1975 and is the result of human intervention. The reforesting of this marshy and completely abandoned area began under the Lorraine government: poplars, pines and cork oaks helped to stabilize the water table

54 top right Another
moment in the lives of
the Maremma
butteri, *who concede
little to modernity
and much to
tradition.*

54 top left
*The Tournament of
the Butteri sees the
Maremma cowboys
competing in various
disciplines relating to
cattle-herding. These
are rough, crude
events like the land in
which they take place.*

54 bottom left
*The San Rossore
estate, a few miles
from Pisa, is a
protected forest of
three thousand
hectares.*
*After having once
belonged to the
emperors, the bishops,
the Medici and the
Houses of Lorraine
and Savoia, it is
today part of the
patrimony of the
president of the
Republic.*

and today the nature reserve provides secure breeding grounds for fallow deer, goats, otters, foxes, badgers and, of course, the wild boar, the symbol of the passion for hunting of the Maremma natives. Not far from the coast, Massa Marittima is another important Maremma town. The irregularly shaped piazza onto which the civic buildings face and the Romanesque cathedral are truly among the architectural treasures of Tuscany. Massa Marittima lies in the center of the Colline Metallifere, or the Metal Hills, which are rich in lead, copper, zinc, alum, pyrites and, above all, silver ore. The mines have created an unusual landscape; as ever, it was the Etruscans who first exploited the resources of the area and there are still signs of their activities, circular shafts in the vicinity in which foundries must have been located. Then, in the Middle Ages, a number of centers began to specialize in the working of metals and since then, with alternating fortune, the hills have continued to supply prime materials. Today many of the mines and quarries have become the target of industrial archaeologists. At Larderello the spectacle of the *soffioni* or, geothermal vents, provides a landscape that Dante might have described. In spite of being channelled and piped now, the *soffioni* still fill the air with clouds of white vapor. The area also boasts a wealth of Etruscan remains. Etruria never had a unified political and administrative configuration and

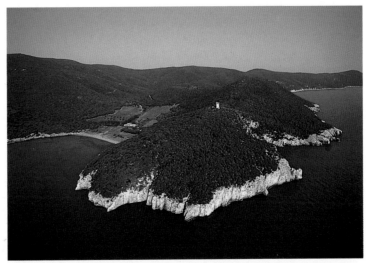

54-55 The Parco dell'Uccellina was, until the beginning of the last century, an area of marshes and scrub suitable only for hunting. Under the government of the House of Lorraine it was systematically re-forested and the water table was regulated. It is now a nature reserve.

55 The Monti dell'Uccellina housed, around the year 1000, Benedictine hermits who built their refuges in the wildest and most isolated areas. Of these only ruins remain, like those of the San Rabano Abbey.

56-57 The coastal pine forest of the Parco dell'Uccellina; below are the Canale dello Scoglietto and in the background, beyond the dunes, the Tyrrhenian Sea. The plantations of stone pines were first established by the House of Lorraine in the 18th century.

58-59 The flora and fauna of the Uccellina are typical of the Mediterranean maquis and the sandy coasts. The park attracts tourists prepared to respect nature and accept its rhythms: visitors may see goats, foxes, badgers or the kings of the Maremma, wild boar.

this gave rise to several city-states. Among the most important were Vetulonia and Populonia. Of the grandeur of both only the faintest of traces remain, but they are sufficient to hint at past glories. Even though much of the devastation was caused by the negligence of humans, it is still an emotional experience to enter the burial mounds, or *edicola,* in which the ancient and mysterious civilization appears to rise again, solemn and silent. Both cities were in sight of the Tyrrhenian; the Tuscan coast is for the most part formed from the detritus brought down over the centuries by the Magra, Serchio, Arno, Cecina, Cornia, Bruna, Ombrone, Albenga and Flora rivers. This explains the sandy beaches separated by rocky spurs that represent a foretaste of the mountains just a few miles away as the crow flies. The other characteristic of the coast is its vegetation: the Mediterranean maquis is rich and varied, and the perfumes of arbutus, gum trees, juniper and mulberry blend with that of saltwater. And while many areas have been raped rather than merely touched by uncontrolled building and the need to provide holiday homes for the crowds of tourists, woods of holm, cork and bay oaks still resist. The dominant species is, however, the stone pine, which represents for the coastal region what the cypress represents for the inland hills, virtually a Tuscan trade-mark. The pines play a more than decorative role: they are an indispensable factor in protecting the inland areas from the salt air, a kind of natural green barrier separating the sea from the hills. The most intensively urbanized area of the coast is undoubtedly Versilia, which is now one long, uninterrupted paean to tourism. What at one time were individual fishing vil-

lages—Forte dei Marmi, Pietrasanta, Camaiore, Foccette and Viareggio—are now a jumbled sequence of bathing *stabilimenti,* hotels, villas and discotheques. Peace and tranquility can be found immediately inland, on the enchanting lake of Massaciuccoli, so dear to Giacomo Puccini, while drama is provided by the Apuan Alps, rising sharply toward the sky. Ever since ancient times, the Apuans have been famous for their marble quarries: the *statuario,* as white as snow, the light blue *bardiglio chiaro* and *bardiglio cupo,* the black and yellow *pavonazzo,* the green *cipollino,* the violet and orange *breccias,* the elegant *arabescato,* with gray veining. It was from here that

62 top Villa di Castello in the vicinity of Florence, once a Medici estate, today houses the Accademia della Crusca, responsible for the defense and diffusion of the Italian language. The garden, designed by Tribolo, features a fountain—seen in the top right—with a bronze group by Ammannati.

62-63 The Castello di Trebbio, between Barberino di Mugello and San Piero a Sieve, was constructed according to designs by Michelozzo. Today it is privately owned.

63 top Villa Mansi at Segromigno (not far from Lucca) dates back to the end of the 16th century, but was restored 200 years later by Filippo Juvara. It is one of the most famous villas in the Lucchese countryside and is surrounded by an English-style park and an Italianate garden overlooked by an airy loggia.

63 center The great frescoed reception hall of Villa Garzoni. The villa is at Collodi, the village close to Pescia famous for being the birthplace of Carlo Lorenzini, the author of Pinocchio.

63 bottom The Medici villa at Poggio a Caiano was constructed in the 15th century by Giuliano da Sangallo. The fashion for country retreats perhaps began with the Medici, who appreciated the possibility of spending a period of rest and relaxation away from the cares of the city. Soon, following their example, all the great families found it necessary to construct sumptuous country houses.

the marble used to build Augustus's Rome was quarried; Michelangelo came here in search of the right blocks for his masterpieces. Today, above all, it is the rich Arab sheikhs who commission palaces that recall the glories of the empire and the Renaissance. Beyond the Apuans, the Garfagnana provides yet another unforgettable landscape. Wild and isolated, cloaked with woodland—covering over 60 percent of the surface, almost a na-tional record—the Garfagnana is a kaleidoscope of gorges, valleys, villages and *pievi*. Within the Orecchiella National Park live deer, goats, mouflon and marmots. While Ludovico Ariosto may have cursed the destiny that brought him here, Giovanni Pascoli chose the Garfagnana as his refuge and last resting place. Before looking at the remaining mountains and the Tuscan islands, we should examine another area of importance in terms of history, culture and nature, the Lunigiana. The name of the area derives from Luni, even though the site now lies in Liguria by a matter of a few hundred yards. In Roman times it was an important town as here cargoes of marble were dispatched to the capital. The port then sank into the sea while the land, carried by the Magra, advanced. The highly evocative ruins reveal city walls and an amphitheater able to accommodate 6,000 spectators. Today the capitals of the marble trade are Massa and Carrara, friendly rivals with a common historical and political back-

ground. All that remains for Luni is the honor of having given its name to a region fundamental from a strategic point of view—Emilia is reached from here via the Cisa Pass. The museum at Pontremoli contains numerous examples of the mysterious stelae statues. The wooded mountain of Pistoia, crowned by the ski resort of Abetone, is the prelude to a landscape that once past the city is, unfortunately, highly industrialized: the fields have become greenhouses and the craft workshops are now factories. A welcome contrast is thankfully provided by the Mugello, the Casentino and Pratomagno. The Mugello, thanks to its benign geography and the political stability it enjoyed over the centuries, is a green valley with fertile terracing, olive groves, and woods of chestnut, holm oak and

beech. The tranquility of the area has always been a great attraction: the villa of Cafaggiolo at San Pietro a Sieve was an ancient fortress that in 1451 Michelozzolo transformed into a residence for the leisure pursuits of Cosimo the Elder, while at Pratolino Francesco dei Medici had a summer residence constructed for his beloved Bianca Capello. Fra Angelico was born at Vicchio, while close by at Vespignano Giotto first saw the light of day. The Casentino, to the north of Arezzo, is the region in which two great rivers, the Arno and the Tiber, both rise. Here again there are towns and villages and centers of religious piety such as Camaldoli Eremo, immersed in unspoiled forests. It was in 1012 that Romualdo and four companions chose the most isolated and silent spot in the Arno Valley in which to pray. The monastery, created as an outpost of the Eremo, achieved its fame and splendor in the 16th century, under the patronage of Lorenzo dei Medici—a member of the Accademia based here—and boasted a prestigious library. Just as suggestive is La Verna, where Saint Francis received the Stigmata.

The peace and serenity of the Casentino turn into bareness, surprise and mystery in the Pratomagno region, the long mountain ridge separating the valley from the Chianti hills. At one time there was a great lake here that gave rise to peculiar eroded rock formations. The *calanchi* emerge from the greenery surrounding the abbey of

64-65 Facing Hidalgo Point, on the extreme tip of Punta Ala, is a handful of rocks scattered across the sea. The largest is known as the Scoglio dello Sparviero, or the Sparrow Hawk Rock; a ruined watchtower is perched on the summit.

65 top and center Punta Ala, an important yachting port and elite tourist resort, and Porto Ercole, which faces a natural bay overlooked by a castle and Spanish fortifications. The demands of modern tourism have led the small fishing village to become an elegant seaside resort clustered around the marina.

65 bottom Another view of the Argentario. These coasts were the object of major conflicts between France and Spain in the 16th century. Spain was the victor and created the Stato dei Presidi. There is still plenty of evidence of the occupation: fortifications dot the area, and ruined watchtowers can be found in the lush vegetation covering the rocks.

66-67 Cape Enfola, to the west of Portoferraio, is one of the many promontories that make the coastline of Elba so irregular. It overlooks Cala Acquaviva, a pearl of sea and sand.

66 top The beach at Fetovaia on the southern coast is one of the most beautiful on the island: white sand and dense Mediterranean vegetation almost reach the transparent water's edge.

67 top The name Portoferraio gives an indication of the town's former occupation. It was here that iron ore was mined and distributed from the Roman era onwards. In this photo you can clearly see, on the right-hand tip of the promontory, the Forte della Stella, with one of its towers converted into a lighthouse.

67 bottom Porto Azzurro; facing the Gulf of Mola on the east coast of Elba is a lively seaside resort, but it is known above all for its grandiose fortress built at Porto Longone on a star-shaped plan by the Spanish in 1603. It was used as a prison.

Vallombrosa from where an almost lunar landscape can be admired. Descending toward Arezzo, at Loro Ciuffenna, is the lacustrine bowl that has proven to be a treasure house of fossils, with elephant, mastodon, hippopotami fossils plus examples of prehistoric flora found here now housed in the museum of palaeontology in Florence. From here you descend toward the Valdichiana: Arezzo is but one of the many unforgettable places. Rising once again toward the Val Tiberiana you reach San Sepolcro, the home town of Piero della Francesca and, further on, Monterchi, where you can admire his most tender and emotional fresco *Madonna del Parto*. To the south, on the other hand, is Cortona, situated on another ridge overlooking the nearby Lake Trasimeno, jewel of a Tuscan art city set in a verdant landscape.

Hills, mountains, plains and beaches, all that remain are the islands. Elba, Gorgona, Pianosa, Montecristo, Giglio and Giannutri, the Tuscan archipelago, were at one time peaks of the Western Alps as can be seen from a distance from the ferry out of Piombino. They rise from the sea steep and green. Their appeal was well known to the Etruscans who not only appreciated natural beauties but were astute enough to know how to exploit them. The iron ore deposits on Elba were also of interest to the Romans, but they preferred the leisure potential of the islands to the labors of mining. The excavations of

the patrician villas are still underway, and each passing season reveals new wonders, usually situated in panoramic positions and equipped with comforts that would be the envy of modern vacationers. The archipelago is so beautiful that after the Romans had departed the islands were by no means left deserted. In fact, they attracted a series of would-be owners, including the Saracen pirates. Elba even became a miniature empire for Napoleon, and it was from here that his last, unsuccessful

venture began. The number of tourists visiting the island is now so great that measures are being taken to protect the environment with recycling programs, restricted use of water and detergents and increased use of bicycles rather than cars. The safeguarding of nature is an imperative at Montecristo, a closed reserve that is prohibited to all visitors after having been a penal colony and a hunting paradise for Vittorio Emanuele II. The other islands are caught between the desire to attract tourism and the need to preserve beaches, cliffs and vegetation. Pines, olives, cypresses, oaks, chestnuts, and a richly varied Mediterranean flora feeds and protects rare bird species, such as the peregrine falcon (on Gorgona and Giannutri); the shearwater (Capraia), migratory birds and a rare gull. Off Montecristo there are also occasional sightings of the monk seal. The islands are a surviving paradise to be defended at all costs in the name of the many areas of Italy ruined by negligence and greed.

68 top left Cala Rossa (top), on the island of Capraia, is hidden by the rocky point of the Zenobito (bottom). The other blood red rocky wall descends to the sea, creating an unusual contrast of colors. The coastline of Capraia is characterized by deep sea caves.

68 top right Giannutri is the southernmost of the Tuscan islands. The bay shown here takes its name from the Capel Rosso knoll, one of three knolls in the area. The others are Monte Mario and the Cannone knoll.

68 bottom right Cala dell'Allume, on the island of Giglio, is one of the most charming bays of the Tuscan archipelago. The island of Giglio owes its exceptionally mild climate to the density of the vegetation: ever since ancient times vineyards have been cultivated here, producing a distinctive wine, the Ansonaco. The local fauna also enjoys a particularly favorable environment—there are abundant wild rabbits, hares, partridges and woodcocks—and the seabed provides memorable excursions for divers.

68-69 The Roman's established a military base on Giannutri, the southernmost island of the Tuscan archipelago; there are numerous remains from the era and the seabed continues to throw up surprises for archaeologists.

69 top The gulls of Capraia. The island is the furthest from the coast (lying over 30 miles from the promontory of Piombino) and from a geological point of view it is of great interest as it is composed of slate, tufa, breccia and basalt: volcanic material, evidence of the archipelago's lively past.

70-71 The Fortezza di San Giorgio dominates a spur of rock on Capraia. Built by the Genoans, it rises almost 110 yards above the level of the sea, clinging to the rock that since ancient times has been the island's natural defense.

72-73 The Calcio Storico *is played on the square in front of Santa Croce in June. The games were originally played in late January, and in 1530 were actually held on the frozen Arno. But not only are the competitors more eager to fight it out in the summer, but there are also considerably more tourists. Nevertheless, the sport remains one of the most deeply and intimately Florentine of events, linked as it is to the four historic quarters of the city. The rules of the* Calcio Storico *are complex and the number of players on the field—27 per team—makes life difficult for the referees. Scuffles are the order of the day, as are the destruction of the beautiful colored costumes, bruises and creative vernacular insults. At the end the winning quarter takes home a calf to be roasted and eaten during the great concluding celebrations.*

"**W**hen the going gets tough the Tuscans get going" would be an appropriate motto for the festivals, tournaments and popular celebrations that animate piazzas throughout the region. There is always a competitive edge, a desire to "put one over" on the opposition, perhaps to reclaim a symbolic trophy, or simply gain the respect and admiration of one's fellow citizens. That the Tuscans are a quarrelsome people is a cliché that has never really been forsworn; fortunately they now channel their aggression into their traditional sports. The beauty of their cities, their language and their sporting passion—in which winning is taken very seriously—are all to the benefit of the tourists crowding the squares during the major events. The vast majority of these spectacles have a long and glorious history or have been revived after a period of neglect. The exception to the rule is the Viareggio Carnival, a money-spinning pageant of allegorical floats that has more in common with the world of business (and the national lotteries) than with folklore. Elsewhere the competitive spirit is still that of the Middle Ages, perhaps tamed somewhat and modified according to the tastes of the Renaissance, when even popular enthusiasm had to have a certain class. Aggression rarely

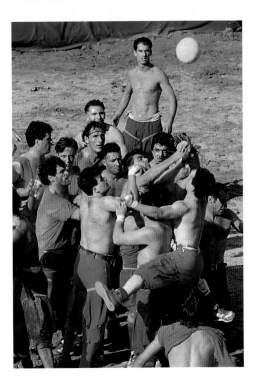

74 top left Lucca, like many other Tuscan cities, has a very strong tournament tradition. This illustration shows the gigantic crossbows that require not only skill but also considerable physical strength.

74 bottom left The Giostra del Saracino in Arezzo. The knights have to try to strike the mannequin representing the Saracen while avoiding his whip, which is loaded with lead weights.

spills over into violence if, that is to say, one ignores the invective and the highly colored cursing that accompanies each and every event and that is frequently amusing and imaginative rather than brutal. Most cities have their own particular sport. In Florence the *sferomachia*, as the *Crusca Dictionary* elegantly defines it, degenerates into the dustiest and most chaotic of football matches imaginable. As Lewis Carroll's Alice might say, "They play without rules, and if there are rules, they ignore them." Four teams represent the four city quarters and the four natural elements (San Giovanni, as the land in green, Santa Croce as water in blue, Santa Maria Novella as fire in red and Santo Spirito as the air in white); there are 27 players on the field for each team, together with a referee (the "Maestro di Campo"), who frequently does not know to which saint he should turn. The spectacle is completed by an extremely complicated set of rules that perhaps only the Florentines themselves really understand, the incitement of the spectators (who at crucial moments do not hesitate to descend from the stands in support of their team) and a pledge of sportsmanship that would appear to be written on the waters of the Arno— soon sworn and even sooner forgotten. At the end of the tournament held in June in Piazza Santa Croce, and preceded by a flag twirling competition, the players are bruised and battered, their beautiful tunics are torn to shreds and the victors celebrate by eating the prize, a white calf. As ever, the losers start planning their revenge. At Pistoia the sport acquires a more noble tone and takes the form of a competition of skill rather than brute force. The *Giostra dell'Orso*, the Bear Joust, held in July in honor of Saint James, dates way back: at one time it was the *Palio dei Barbieri*, a breakneck race involving the entire city and preceded by violent games on the borderline of legality. Five hundred years later the revived event has become more civilized. In Piazza Duomo, the 12 horsemen representing the various city parishes attempt to strike a target in the shape of a bear—the symbol of the city of Pistoia—with the tips of their lances. Again the main event is set off

74 right On the first Sunday in September Arezzo echoes to the sound of drums and trumpets announcing the herald, who reads the proclamation of the Giostra del Saracino. In the afternoon the weapons of the competitors are blessed in front of the local parish churches, and after a parade the tournament begins in Piazza Grande.

75 The origins of the
Giostra del Saracino
held in Arezzo date
back to the 12th
century. The knights
"running the lance"
represent the quarters
of Porta
Sant'Andrea, Porta
Crucifera, Porta del
Foro and Porta
Santo Spirito.

by characters in 15th-century dress, drummers, flag twirlers, dames and knights. Historical revival is also the name of the game at Arezzo with the *Giostra del Saracino*, the Saracen Joust. This event celebrates the knightly tournaments of the Middles Ages held to mark the arrival in the city of important personages and in which the local gentlemen competed for the usual *palio* or banner. Today the competitors are representatives of the city quarters and enact the joust in the main square, Piazza Grande. The target is a marionette, a dummy representing the hated Saracen and capable of extracting his own revenge by striking an inexpert knight with a whip of weighted balls. A regatta on the waters of the Arno is the main attraction of Pisa's Saint Ranieri celebrations held between the 16th and the 17th of July. During the night thousands of oil lamps are lit along the riverbanks, on the balconies of the buildings (together with the *biancheria*, a white wooden support) and on miniature boats. With all other illumination extinguished the river glows like a long tongue of fire descending slowly toward the sea. The following day the city's valiant oarsmen evoke the era in which Pisa contended control of the Mediterranean with Venice, Genoa and Amalfi in the *Regata delle Repubbliche Marinare.*

76 left The Regatta of the Marine Republics at Pisa is a riot of sumptuous costumes—like that of the doge with his ermine cloak and of the young lady—and competitive spirit, with teams from Pisa, Venice, Genoa and Amalfi engaged on the waters of the Arno.

76 right The detonation of the wagon on Easter morning in front of the Duomo reveals the fortunes of the coming year for the Florentines. The powder is ignited by the "dove," a rocket that departs from the high altar in the cathedral.

77 The Regatta of the Marine Republics attracts thousands of spectators to Pisa, but the lights of San Ranieri illuminate the city's most heartfelt festival. During the night of June 16, the street lamps are switched off and small oil lamps trace the outlines of the building and the banks of the river. As dusk falls thousands of little boats carrying lamps are launched toward the sea.

The sea again figures strongly in the *Palio Marinaro* at Livorno, while the citizens of Sansepolcro re-enact the *Palio delle Balestre*, another event with medieval roots. However, the greatest and the most famous of these sporting occasions is undoubtedly the *Palio* held in Siena. The thousands of tourists crowding the Piazza del Campo and the millions of television spectators see but the briefest of races around the square, a kaleidoscope of galloping horses, nervous jockeys and feverishly excited *contradaioli*, or local supporters. For anybody born beyond the shadow of the Mangia Tower it must be very difficult to comprehend exactly what lies behind the apparently straightforward event: months and months of preparations, discussions, arguments and reconciliation, rivers of money that pass from hand to hand, miles of colored cloth, curses and blessings, banquets and secret negotiations, friendships broken and alliances sealed. The animal rights activists protest, hopelessly pleading for the suppression of a sport in which the horse is the undisputed king. They cry over the poor beasts injured on the San Martino Curve, but not a tear is shed for the jockeys who if they fall are lucky to be treated. Their mounts, on the other hand, are more cosseted—spoiled, tamed and fed with love—than

78 Thousands of pages have been written about the Palio of Siena, and yet for those born beyond the shadow of the Mangia Tower it is difficult to comprehend the passion and fervor of the Sienese for this competition. At the top, the banner of the Selva; below, the blessing of the horse of one of the contrade in the parish church.

78-79 and 79 top
This wagon, drawn
by four oxen, carries
the Palio banner: it is
a stirring moment in
which every self-
respecting Sienese
citizen is already
anticipating the
honor of being a
member of the
victorious contrada.
In the large photo, a
contrada member
proudly bearing the
banner of "his"
Tartuca.

79 right During the
day of the race, even
the contrade that are
not taking part in
the Palio have their
moment of glory. This
photo shows a member
of the Contrada del
Gallo.

the most fortunate of crown princes. A veterinary surgeon is more esteemed than any professor of human medicine and at the end of their careers the heroic steeds' final destination is not the abattoir but comfortable farms on the Sienese hills. As pampered pensioners, they possibly recall the days in which the place of honor, in church as well as at the banqueting table, was reserved for them. In their mind's eye they will may still see the colors of the *contrada* they carried to victory or the pennant dedicated to the Madonna that their feats conquered. The Tuscan taste for celebration manifests itself not only in the major tournaments; in Florence, for example, Easter would hardly be Easter without the *Scoppio del Carro*, an ancient propitiatory ceremony (dating back to the first Crusade): the detonation of the dove that sets off the fireworks in the wagon in front of the Duomo is a source of interminable discussion. A whole-hearted explosion announces a happy and prosperous year, while a damp squib augurs a sad and ill-favored time for all. In September the Virgin's birthday is marked by the *Festa delle Rificolone*—crepe paper lanterns illuminate the San Nicolò Bridge while boats descend the Arno. Other festivals celebrate local produce such as the ones at Impruneta or Colonnata. In terms of the delights of the palate, no visit to Tuscany would be complete without sampling some of the local delicacies. The fertility of the countryside and a gastronomic tradition based on the excellence of its natural

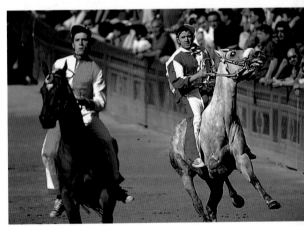

81 During the race friendships and family ties go by the boards in the name of competition. Occasionally corruption raises its ugly head: it is not unknown for a contrada to "buy off" the jockey of one of its rivals. All's fair in love, war and the Palio of Siena.

82-83 The San Martino corner rounded during the Palio at Siena is rightly feared by even the most expert and audacious of jockeys. It is here that the most spectacular and dangerous falls occur, dangerous for both the horses and their riders. The padding intended to provide protection is of little help.

81

ingredients have given rise to some flavorsome cooking. Olive oil takes pride of place and a slice of *panunto* (seasoned bread), flavored with garlic is one of the tastiest of foods one could find. The Chianina cattle provide the renowned *Fiorentine*, thick T-bone steaks to be cooked on charcoal grills, while the heights of fish cuisine are reached with the *caciucco*, from Livorno. Then there are various kinds of sheep's cheese: the *pecorino* from Siena, the *ravaggiolo* of the Mugello and the *marzolino*. These should all be washed down with a glass

of Tuscan wine, Brunello from Montalcino, Vin Nobile from Montepulciano, Vernaccia from San Gimignano, or Chianti, perhaps the world's most famous wine. The name "Chianti" derives from the Etruscan *Clante-i* and was originally used to identify a product of high quality. In 1924 a consortium was set up to protect the identity and character of the wine of the Chianti region and restrict the use of its symbol, a black cockerel on a gold background. As early as the late 19th century, however, Bettino Ricasoli, the father of the Chianti wine culture, had established the parameters for identifying the real McCoy: seven tenths Sangiovese (body and color), two tenths Canaiolo (bouquet and smoothness) and a tenth of Trebbiano and Malvasia (acidity and refinement). It is still a winning recipe, in spite of attempts at imitation so numerous that Harold Acton was to say that if all the wine sold as Chianti was produced in the region, then the Chianti hills would have to extend as far as the steppes of Central Asia.

The countryside has also nurtured a rich craft tradition that has to some extent resisted encroaching industrialization. Leather, paper and wickerwork are still produced in Florence, and the city also supports a flourishing restoration trade. In the region of Volterra alabaster is the prime material for statues, while on the Apuan hills marble is worked. At Scarperia in the Mugello the art of the knife makers is alive and well. The trade has ancient origins and in 1538 was regulated by a statute. Then there are the antique fairs like those of Arezzo and Cortona, justly famous throughout the world.

From the Roman *castrum* to the city of today: historical and artistic developments have led to Florence becoming an immensely complex urban center that is by no means easy to manage, so much so that each and every innovation is greeted with interminable argument. The Roman city plan (the *cardo* corresponds to the modern-day Via degli Speziali and Via Strozzi, and the *decumano* to the junction of Vias Roma and Calimala) was overlaid with an extremely random and varied medieval structure, while this itself has been altered by the Renaissance structures and the demolition work of the last century performed in the name of a so-called restoration of the city center. The result is that today those who arrive in Florence expecting to find a great open-air museum will instead find a living, breathing and mutating city, as is only right and proper. The regional capital of Tuscany has been spared, at least in part, the sad fate of Venice, which is paying for its status as an artistic jewel in terms of a shrinking, aging population. Prisoners of the tourists, the Venetians are gradually surrendering to the inevitable, crossing Ponte della Libertà and settling in exile in Mestre. Under siege, but resolute, the Florentines are putting up

86-87 The center of Florence, dominated by the dome of Santa Maria del Fiore and the smaller one of San Lorenzo. Behind the curtain of buildings marking the course of the Arno can be seen the medieval street plan of the city.

87 top Ponte Vecchio, Ponte Santa Trinità and Ponte alla Carraia follow one after the other over the waters of the Arno. Miraculously spared the destruction of the Second World War, the Ponte Vecchio today houses famous jewelers' shops but was once the city's meat market.

87 right Probably begun according to designs by Arnolfo di Cambio in 1294 and completed in the last century with a mediocre "historical" facade, Santa Croce is the pantheon of the national heroes; here are buried Alfieri, Machiavelli, Michelangelo, Vasari, Rossini and Ugo Foscolo, who in his poem Sepolcri, *sang the praises of the inspiration behind the church.*

88 left
The monument to Dante, perhaps the most famous Florentine citizen, by Enrico Pazzi in Piazza Santa Croce. The square has housed, since ancient times, great crowds, some to hear the preaching of Saint Bernardino of Siena, others attracted by various games and tournaments.

strenuous resistance: they may have ceded the city center to fast food and pizza joints but they refuse to allow intrusions into their daily lives. Walk through one of the street markets and you will still hear the distinctive local speech patterns. Pass an evening at the Pergola theater or one of the local nightclubs and you will realize that the tourists have yet to conquer this particular city. In the Florentine workshops authentic artisans work not for the passing Americans happy to pick up an industrial reproduction of a Renaissance *putto*, but for the great families restoring the palazzi of their forebears piece by piece. The scholars at the National Library, the Laurenziana and Mediceo-Ricciardiana Library, at the Marucelliana, at the Viesseux and at the Accademia della Crusca are working for the benefit of Italian culture, certainly not for the benefit of the all-inclusive tour visits. The *Opificio delle Pietre Dure* does not sell lapis lazuli necklaces, but restores precious objects. This all goes to show that you cannot expect to visit Florence for a couple of days of ritual sightseeing and leave thinking that you have done it all. You could hardly say you know New York without having walked in Central Park or that you know Paris without ever having dined in a bistro. Similarly Florence should be seen as a proud and vital city refusing to live on its past laurels and determined to continue its thousand-year development, to the chagrin of those who would prefer to see it placed in a glass museum case.

88 top right Built by Michelozzo in the middle of the 15th century, the Palazzo Medici-Riccardi today houses the prefecture. The courtyard contains Bandinelli's statue of Orpheus, set off by the beguiling perspective of the arcades.

88 center right The Florentine lily, symbol of the city council since the time of the Medici, appears on the pediment over the entrance to the Palazzo Vecchio.

88 bottom right Created according to the wishes of Eleonora, the wife of Cosimo I, the Boboli Gardens mirror late Renaissance taste, with grottoes, walks, fountains, vast lawns and clipped hedges. This photo shows Neptune's Pool.

89 Piazza della Signoria is graced by a wealth of sculpture. In the foreground is Baccio Bandinelli's Hercules and Cacus; then comes the copy of Michelangelo's David and, in the background, Ammannati's Neptune Fountain. A circle in front of the fountain marks the spot where Savonarola was hanged and set on fire.

90 *At dusk two of the symbols of Florence stand out, the Palazzo della Signoria and the church of Santo Spirito. The last fruit of the genius of Brunelleschi, Santo Spirito displays an austere and unusually simple facade. The dome and the campanile were added at later dates.*

91-94 *Ponte Vecchio seems like a veritable city, an agglomeration of buildings stacked up on the ancient spans. Today it is famous for its jewelers' shops, but it was once the realm of the Florentine butchers.*

95 The bulk of the Duomo of Florence emerges against the city skyline. The audacity of Brunelleschi's dome, a masterpiece of stability and lightness, stunned the artist's contemporaries. It sits alongside Giotto's Tower which, with its perfect proportions, is further evidence of the genius of Angelo di Bondone, the shepherd turned artist.

96 In the midst of the uniform street plan of Siena, miraculously intact after so many centuries, rises the great bulk of the Duomo with, in the background, the red brick bowl of the Piazza del Campo.

Sealed as it is within its city walls, and set in one of the most beautiful landscapes in the world, Siena has had the privilege of maintaining intact its original appearance. It is at night, when the shops are closed and the illuminated signs are switched off that wandering the arched streets, you appreciate the unique qualities of the city. Privilege has its price of course: it is difficult to adapt to modern life when every stone is a part of history. The original nucleus, perched on three hills that meet at the Croce del Travaglio, has been influenced by the morphology of the landscape, and even Pizza del Campo owes its inclination to the natural slope: a broad terra-cotta red bowl amidst a labyrinth of streets in which

openings are rare due to the need to utilize space to the best effect while remaining as far as possible within the beloved city walls. Siena continues to enjoy a degree of isolation; reaching the city by train, for example, is an enterprise best left to the most patient of travelers. The highway linking it to Florence passes through an area of rare beauty and plugs it into the national motorway network, but it has to be said that much of the appeal of the city lies in its remaining tranquil and a little disdainful, with that civic pride that the knocks of contemporary life have failed to dent.

97 bottom left The shadow of the Mangia Tower is traced on the buildings and the pavement of the Piazza del Campo. The elegant noble palazzi that surround the piazza were built according to severe norms established by the council at the end of the 13th century to preserve the dignity of the city's showpiece square.

97 top right The 14th-century Palazzo Salimbeni, the home of the Monte dei Paschi di Siena bank, has a Gothic Revival appearance thanks to the 19th-century modifications made by Giuseppe Partini.

97 bottom right The color of the houses and the roofs of Siena is warm and homogeneous; it recalls the tones of the Crete, the surrounding countryside, in a perfect fusion of art and nature.

98 top Seen from the walls of Lucca, the garden of the Palazzo Pfanner shows the elaborate taste of the 17th century. The palazzo now houses a costume museum.

98-99 Piazza del Mercato, one of Lucca's best-loved squares, cannot hide its origins: during Roman times it was the site of the amphitheater and it has preserved its perfect oval plan. To the right runs the Fillungo, a long street that almost bisects the historic town center.

LUCCA

The origins of Lucca are mysterious. The Celtic-Ligurian derivation of its name indicates that it may be pre-Roman. *Luk* was the term used to describe a marshy area and, in fact, at one time there was the ancient Lake of Bientina in the area that occasionally flooded the surrounding countryside. Today, on the other hand, Lucca is one of the most pleasant Italian cities in which to live, not only for the beauty of its palazzi and churches, the urbanity of its compact and harmonious city center and its truly human dimensions, but also for the extraordinary setting in which it lies. The Luccesian countryside, with its hills of vineyards and olive groves punctuated by lavish villas, is the perfect counterpoint to the provincial capital itself. It is as open as Lucca is closed inside its massive walls and bastions; as dedicated to leisure as Lucca is industrious and founded, from the earliest times, on a solid mercantile class. The solidity of wool and silk did not impede Lucca from acquiring a feminine quality, tied as it is to the angelic face of Ilaria del Carretto, wife of Paolo Guinigi, who rests in the Duomo of San Martino portrayed by Jacopo della Quercia in one of the most serene and "affectionate" works in the history of art. Ilaria and the beauty of love is at the heart of any visit to Lucca.

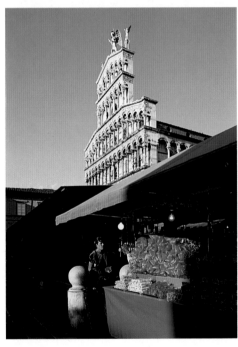

99 Piazza San Michele in Foro is one of the key squares in Lucca. More central than the Duomo, with its imposing facade crowned by the statue of the archangel, the San Michele church was built on the foundations of an 8th-century temple.

100 top left The small church of Santa Maria della Spina on the banks of the Arno derives its name from a relic of Christ's Crown of Thorns now in the church of Santa Chiara. Pinnacles, niches, cusps and arcades make it a jewel of Gothic architecture.

100 bottom left Pisa and the Arno seen from the Torre dell'Orologio. The banks of the Arno at Pisa, lined by sober palazzi, are illuminated during the San Ranieri celebrations when every balcony is decorated with a line of small lamps.

*L*igurians, Ionians and Etruscans all have claims on the founding of Pisa. However, even though today the city is to be found some miles from the coast, the sea is its true raison d'être. Between the years 1000 and 1300 the development of its maritime power was quite remarkable. The Pisans fought against the Saracens, they participated in the Crusades and conquered Sardinia, Corsica and Majorca. And at the same time they transformed their city into a work of art. Today the ancient battles have been forgotten. The city does, however, retain its cultural position: the Pisan university is one of the oldest in Italy, with a supremacy recognised in Roman law. The Scuola Normale Superiore, founded by Napoleon and reorganized by Leopold II in 1846, is a point of departure—or arrival—for the most brilliant minds in the country. The University of Pisa has attracted Alfieri, Leopardi, Byron, Shelley and Elizabeth Barret Browning and embodies a strongly rooted cultural tradition nurtured under the protective wing of Galileo Galilei, to whom modern physics owes the scientific method of investigation still used today that integrates the results of experiments and observations and is fundamental in the formulation of theories. This method might well have had its origins in the very heart of the city, below the great bronze incense lamp hanging in the Duomo, Galileo's lamp.

100 right The statue of Cosimo I in Piazza dei Cavalieri, the heart of the ancient republican city. Palazzo dei Cavalieri, rebuilt by Giorgio Vasari for the Order of Saint Stephen, is the home of the Scuola Normale Superiore.

101 The Piazza dei Miracoli complex at Pisa—the Baptistery, the Duomo, the Tower and the Camposanto—is a monument dedicated to God, but also a memorial to the wealth achieved by the city thanks to maritime trading, the expeditions to the Middle East and North Africa and its victories over the infidels and its business rivals.

OTHER ARTISTIC CENTERS

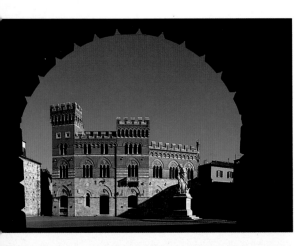

There are four Tuscan Queens, Florence, Pisa, Siena and Lucca. But the ladies-in-waiting are no less worthy of love, consideration and respect. One by one virtually all of the cities in the region have played leading roles in political and artistic events, but history has called on just a few of them to emerge leaving the others in an aura of tranquility that has nothing in common with mediocrity. Taken one by one, Livorno, Grosseto, Massa, Carrara, Arezzo and Pistoia have nothing to fear in comparison with other artistic centers, not only in Italy, but throughout the world. Each of these living cities has certain distinguishing characteristics: at Livorno it is the sea; at Grosseto it is the Maremma and the Etruscan civilization; Massa and Carrara are the undisputed capitals of the marble industry; Arezzo is the center of the goldsmiths' trade; and Pistoia is the capital of one of the wealthiest and most industrialized areas of Tuscany. If they do have to follow a half step behind the four queens, they nevertheless maintain their noble status with pride, frequently in close contact with the extraordinarily varied surrounding countryside in which each church, each house and each farm has its own history and is ready to recount it.

102 top left Piazza Dante is the heart of Grosseto, enclosed within its massive walls. In the center is a statue of Leopold II erected in recognition of the grand duke's efforts to control malaria, a disease endemic to the Maremma. In the background is the Palazzo della Provincia.

102 bottom left The sumptuous Palazzo Cybo Malaspina at Massa, decorated with 18th-century white stucco. The palazzo is in Piazza Aranci, which takes its name from the orange trees lending it shade.

102-103 The Canale della Fortezza Nuova constitutes the so-called "New Venice," a 17th-century quarter with buildings destined for sailors and fishermen. Proceeding along the canal one reaches the Fortezza Vecchia, built by Antonio da Sangallo the Younger in the first half of the 16th century.

103 top Piazza Grande at Arezzo, surrounded by buildings that summarize the history of the city, from the Palazzo del Tribunale to that of the Fraternità dei Laici and the Logge by Giorgio Vasari.

103 top right Carrara—in this photo a palazzo on Piazza Alberica—is the world marble capital. The city's quarries supply the brilliant white statuario, Michelangelo's favorite material. Behind the city rise the Apuan Alps, where the landscape appears to be covered in snow thanks to the quarries.

103 bottom right The portico of the Ospedale del Ceppo at Pistoia is decorated with a polychrome terra-cotta frieze from the Della Robbia studio; it illustrates the seven works of mercy.

104 top Famous throughout the world, The Wounded Chimera of Bellerofonte, *also known as the* Arezzo Chimera, *dates back to the 5th century BC. Discovered in 1555, it was restored by Benvenuto Cellini. In the Etruscan era Arezzo was an important center for bronze work.*

104 bottom The slim Etruscan statuettes found at Brolio in the Val di Chiana represent a warrior and a lady; they presumably date back to around 550 BC and probably served as supports for a piece of wooden furniture.

The most recent research into Etruscan art has led to two fundamental considerations: first, that it cannot be considered as having unitary, homogeneous characteristics, and second, that it is an artistic phenomenon owing much to the Hellenistic tradition. It was principally the cities of southern Etruria—those that are for the most part to be found in the Lazio region today—that enjoyed a political and cultural hegemony; the monumental tombs of Cerveteri are convincing proof of that fact. The art of painting developed at Tarquinia, while Vulci specialized in ceramics and Veio in sculpture. The influence of this series of art and craft specializations reached as far North as Volterra and Fiesole. This was in the 7th century BC, a period in which the Hellenic influence was extremely strong as Greek artists were employed by the leading figures of the Etruscan cities, anxious to perpetuate their family histories. It was a period of great splendor that only began to show signs of decline in the difficult political atmosphere of the 5th century.

During the 4th century a degree of revival led to the establishment of other artistic schools: decorators of alabaster urns at Volterra and of ceramic urns in other large and small cities. Etruscan ceramics are worthy of more detailed discussion. *Bucchero* was typical of Cerveteri, where vases and urns were produced with very thin walls and decoration of clearly Greek derivation. Ceramic production spread through-

out the region and the influence of foreign artists allowed extremely high-quality objects to be produced. The ceramic artists were not, however, well-known figures (with the exception of Aristonoto), but paid craftsmen, generally employed to reproduce the established, traditional stylistic motifs that appealed to an aristocracy eager to seal their place in history. This situation created the conditions for the formation of other centers of specialization: funerary architecture at Cerveteri, monumental painting at Tarquinia and sculpture at Vulci. The Guarnacci Etruscan Museum at Volterra provides a useful overview of the art of this mysterious civilization. The museum contains the funerary trappings found in the numerous necropoli of the region: around 700 tufa, terra-cotta and alabaster urns, including the well-known example with decorative elements depicting a couple of presumed newlyweds. There are also stelae celebrating warlike virtues and cinerary urns from the Villanovian era. Jewelry, coins and small bronzes are testimony to the variety of influences and styles that combined in this fascinating period of artistic expression. The Archaeological Museum at Arezzo is equally interesting and contains a number of Roman exhibits and finds from the tombs around Populonia, Vetulonia and Sovana. The "Romanization" of Tuscia was rapid and extensive, although evidence of the republican and imperial splendors were frequently covered by and incorporated into the

105 top A bust of the young Augustus conserved in the Guarnacci Etruscan Museum at Volterra. Even though political events had put the city in danger on several occasions, in the era of Imperial Rome Volterra continued to enjoy a full cultural life. The construction of the Roman theater dates from this period.

105 bottom The sarcophagus of Larthia in polychrome terra-cotta discovered at Chiusi and conserved in the Archaeological Museum in Florence. This museum, housed in the Palazzo della Crocetta, is one of the most important of its kind and also features Greek and Roman sculpture and Egyptian and numismatic sections.

medieval cities. The archaeological digs at Fiesole brought to light a large Roman theater and remains of thermal baths from the 1st century AD, and there are also traces of large monumental complexes at Volterra and Roselle. In the latter case there are remains of the city walls, the forum, noble houses, thermal baths and an amphitheater, evidence of a wealthy and glorious past. On the island of Elba excavations are still underway to bring to light Roman villas decorated with precious mosaics while the Maremma conceals, amidst its Etruscan remains, sumptuous noble residences. Perhaps the most evocative reminder of the epoch is to be found in the center of Lucca, in the beautiful Piazza Anfiteatro whose oval form has been respected by the constructions of successive eras and in which traces of the tribunes can still be seen: a perfect example of architectural integration. It was in the Middle Ages that Tuscany assumed a pivotal role in the history of Italian art. The phenomenon is all the more interesting in that it involved not only the major cities, such as Florence, Lucca, Siena and Pisa, but also the

smaller centers. Almost perfectly intact medieval towns such as San Gimignano and Monteriggioni are clear evidence of this fact. The dominant art form was architecture with differing stylistic elements from one area to the next and various influences being imported from France and Lombardy. In the case of the church of San Miniato al Monte in Florence, the Florentine Romanesque style has clearly been influenced by early Christian motifs, with the luminous facade in white-and-green marble anticipating the geometrical rigor of much of the art of the city. Equally characteristic are San Giovanni, the baptistery mentioned by Dante, with its severe austerity and the Badia Fiesolana. Emphasized by the green-and-white Prato marble, massive yet at the same time airy with its pyramidal roof, the Baptistery at Florence has been enriched over the centuries with innumerable works of art. The magnificent bronze doors, the fruit of the genius of Andrea Pisano (the south door) and Lorenzo Ghiberti (the doors to the north and the west, the "Gates of Paradise," according to Michelangelo), the 13th-century mosaics and the *Christ* by Coppo di Marcovaldo are all set in a relatively compact space and represent a summation of Florentine art.

107 left Poppi, in the Casentino, is celebrated for its Palazzo Pretorio, once the castle of the Guidi Counts. It houses an important library, the strict custodian of manuscripts, incunabula and rare books.

107 top right San Miniato al Monte is considered to be the most beautiful example of the Florentine Romanesque. The facade, with its white-and-green marble, stands tall and luminous on Monte delle Croci and is visible from much of the city.

107 bottom right The Badia Fiesolana, the origins of which lie prior to the year 1000, has preserved its original facade with the typical two-color geometric decorations. Alongside is the former convent housing the European University.

108 left Tradition attributes the construction of the campanile of the Duomo of Pisa to Bonanno. The tower was originally designed to be much taller, but subsidence halted building work for almost a century and then restricted the overall height.

108 top The apse in the Duomo at Pisa is, like the facade, by Rainaldo, who continued the work of Buscheto. The architect is remembered in an inscription at the base of the first order on the facade; he is defined as a prudens operator et ipse magister (brilliant architect and master).

108-109 The facade of the Duomo is considered to be the model for an architectural genre. The motif of the superimposed loggias is Lombard in origin, but Rainaldo enriched it with intricate intaglio work, cornices and inlay decoration.

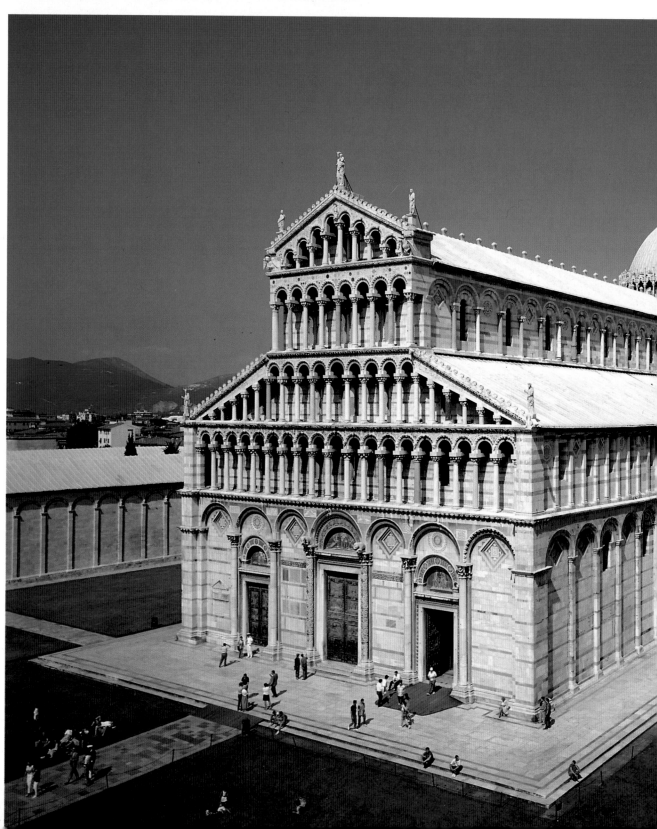

109 top The pulpit in the Duomo at Pisa, sculpted between 1302 and 1310, is one of Giovanni Pisano's greatest works. The nine panels supported by columns feature figures and allegorical groups and achieve heights of intense drama animated by a vehemence that was to be seen in Donatello's later works.

The other major Romanesque thread in Tuscany is to be found at Pisa and Lucca and involves the development of Lombard themes, revised with supreme elegance and the addition of Arabic motifs. The latter were the fruit, in the case of Pisa, of the city's maritime connections. Buscheto, the architect of the first version of the Duomo at Pisa at the end of the 11th century, took on the classical inheritance and reinterpreted it, setting the tone for a number of other buildings, such as the churches of San Frediano and Sant'Alessandro at Lucca. Pisa's Campo dei Miracoli can be said to be the archetype of Pisan Romanesque architecture in spite of having been constructed in different periods and with the contribution of various artists. During the Longobard era Lucca had enjoyed the privilege of being the ducal seat and the capital of the region, a period of great splendor. Shortly after the year 1000, early in the era of the free communes, it was the setting for some of Tuscany's most beautiful Romanesque architecture, rivaled only by that of Pisa. The codified forms of Buscheto were simplified: San Martino, San Michele and Sant'Alessandro have a coherence and severity barely disturbed by decoration. Subsequent buildings saw an increasing use of chromatism and toward the middle of the 12th century new facades began to be applied to the oldest churches. Lucca is also notable for its country churches, the *pievi* of Gattaiola, Santa Maria del Giudice and Loppia, monuments to popular piety. The Romanesque style

109 right The magnificent Piazza dei Miracoli is worthy of detailed examination. Each statue, each column and each piece of decoration has its place in a very precise decorative and spatial structure and contributes to a masterpiece of formal harmony.

110 top left *Set close to the San Colombano bastion, San Martino, the Duomo of Lucca, was perhaps founded by San Frediano in the 6th century, but the building we know today dates back to the 11th through the 13th centuries. It contains one of the world's most beautiful works of art, the tomb of Ilaria del Carretto by Jacopo della Quercia.*

110 bottom *The mosaic high on the facade of San Frediano at Lucca is attributed to the pupils of Berlinghieri. It depicts the Ascension of Christ and in spite of the heavy-handed restoration of the last century, it retains the plasticity and coloring typical of the Lucchese masters.*

was also a feature of the architecture of Pistoia, with a distinct local variation seen in monuments such as the Duomo, Sant'Andrea, San Bartolomeo in Pantano, San Giovanni Fuorcivitas and San Pietro as well as many minor churches in the city and the surrounding countryside. Sacred architecture was complemented and supported by the flourishing art of sculpture, itself influenced by French Gothic and the rich Lombard tradition. With the work of Bonanno (the doors of the Duomo at Pisa, the sculptures of the Duomo at Lucca and the *pievi* of Arezzo and Pistoia), Gugliemo, Gruamonte and Biduino—who left traces of his art above all at Lucca—the ground was prepared for the greatest sculptor of the 13th century, Nicola Pisano. Coming from Puglia and the Federician court and having a classical background, Pisano rejected once and for all the Byzantine tradition, inventing a brand new sculptural language that laid the basis for a more human and heroic art form. The pulpit in the baptistery at

110 top right *The church of San Michele at Lucca dates from the late Lucchese Romanesque period, plastic, solemn, yet extremely light. The luminosity of the marble is also found in the campanile and contrasts with the severe atmosphere of the interior.*

110 center right *Another view of the Duomo of Lucca: this shot reveals the richness of the apse and the complexity of the structure.*

111 *The Duomo of Pistoia has extremely ancient origins; it was rebuilt in the 12th century and in the 14th century a portico was added to the facade. The campanile was originally a Longobard watchtower and in the late 13th century was transformed with the construction of the three final loggias in the Pisan Romanesque style.*

Pisa is a truly a fundamental work in the history of Italian art: Pisano drew on models from ancient sculpture, discovering a certain dignity and culture that were eventually to lead toward humanism. He also made his presence felt at Lucca, with the relief sculptures on the lunettes of the doors of San Martino, and he directly influenced a whole generation of artists. Among his followers was his son Giovanni, who in the pulpit of the church of Sant'Andrea at Pistoia achieved an incomparable degree of expressive drama. The sculptor was finally free to put his forms into motion, to see them live and breathe. The second pupil of and successor to Nicola Pisano, Arnolfo di Cambio, developed a different form of classicism that tended toward a virtually timeless staticity. In 1295 Arnolfo assumed the duties of civil and military architect of the city of Florence and designed a number of monuments that represented the origins of important stylistic developments: Santa Croce, Santa Maria del Fiore and the Palazzo della Signoria (Palazzo Vecchio). For many centuries the latter was to represent the archetypal Florentine palazzo, while the horizontality and breadth of Santa Maria del Fiore were to form the basic structure around which the genius of Brunelleschi operated.

112-113 The 13th-century church of Santa Croce is attributed to Arnolfo di Cambio.

113 left The design of the Palazzo Vecchio in Florence is attributed to Arnolfo di Cambio, who began work in 1299, incorporating the ancient tower of the Foraboschi into the building. On the right can be seen the

Loggia dei Lanzi, a fine example of Florentine Gothic architecture.

113 top right The chancel, illuminated by stained-glass windows designed by Agnolo Gaddi, houses a large crucifix by a follower of Giotto and, on the walls, frescoes by Gaddi representing the Legend of the True Cross.

113 center right In the upper part of the immense Salone dei Cinquecento the grand duke of Tuscany held audiences, surrounded by Vasari's frescoes celebrating the history of Florence.

113 bottom right The first courtyard of the Palazzo Vecchio features a wealth of decoration: the fountain, the sculptures and the plants transform the space into a kind of winter garden.

The penetration of styles arriving from France was also responsible for a renewal of architectural languages. Monastic buildings, such as San Galgano or the abbey of Sant'Antimo, are examples of this mutation. In spite of the absence of its roof—which perhaps to our eyes makes it all the more suggestive—the abbey of San Galgano marks the union of Gothic "verticalism" with a Romanesque rationalism. The medley of styles is even more evident in the Duomo of Siena. This building represents a kind of summation of Sienese art, achieved through the combined work of architects, painters and sculptors from different backgrounds. The classicism of Nicola Pisano, triumphant in the pulpit, the Gothic of Giovanni Pisano, the decorations of the floor and the two-tone interior theme all contribute to a composition with few rivals. In the church of Santa Maria Novella in Florence there is evidence of a trend that could be defined as humanist. This solemn breadth, based on a human rather than divine scale, can also be seen in civil buildings such as the public palazzi of Siena and Volterra and the Bargello in Florence. At Siena, on the Piazza del Campo, the ancient *Campus Fori*, rose the palazzo designed to celebrate the splendors of local government, while on all sides rose the noble residences of the Piccolomini, the Sansedoni and the Alessi families, all built to precise, codified rules dedicated to the greater glory of the municipality. At Lucca civil building was to develop above all under the dominion of the good Paolo Guinigi, with the Villa Guinigi constructed

114-115 The Duomo of Siena is the product of the talent of innumerable artists who starting in the first half of the 13th century applied themselves to the glory of the Virgin to whom the building is dedicated. This illustration clearly shows the two-tone marble motif found throughout.

115 top Another view of the Duomo. The roof in the foreground hides the walls of the extension of the church that was never completed.

115 bottom The interior of the Duomo is extremely richly decorated, in an almost Oriental style, emphasized by the marble dressings, carvings and the decoration of the ceiling vaults.

116 top Set like a precious jewel in a valley close to Montalcino is the abbey of Sant'Antimo founded, according to popular legend, by Charlemagne. Today it is only inhabited by a small group of French monks, but each Sunday the church is filled with the faithful, attracted by the tranquility of the site and the Gregorian chants.

116 bottom The upper part of the marble facade of Santa Maria Novella in Florence was designed by Leon Battista Alberti (as was the portal), and harmonizes extraordinarily well with the lower section that is still clearly Gothic in style with Romanesque overtones.

117 top The crucifix by Coppo di Marcovaldo, carved together with his son Salerno in 1275, is to be found in the Duomo of Pistoia. Coppo di Marcovaldo has been recognized as the master of Cimabue: the suffering Christ is surrounded by scenes from the Passion.

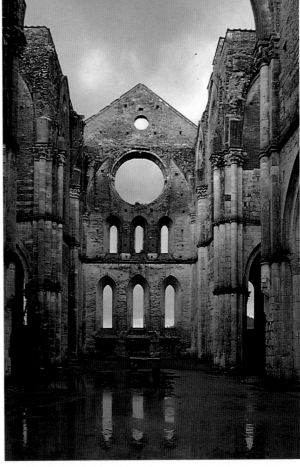

117 bottom San Galgano, now reduced to evocative ruins, was founded by a noble knight who chose the Sienese hills in which to spend his last years as a hermit. Its decline began in the 15th century and less than a hundred years later the disaster was complete.

118 The frescoes narrating the Stories of Santa Fina in the Collegiata at San Gimignano were executed by Domenico Ghirlandaio and are to be found in the Renaissance setting of the chapel by Giuliano and Benedetto da Maiano.

for the nobleman's out-of-town leisure and numerous palazzi built within the city walls. In the meantime the foundations were also being laid for a "revolution" in painting with a breakaway from the Byzantine stylistic motifs; Giorgio Vasari summed up this evolution when speaking of Giotto: "The art of painting changed from Greek to Latin." Others had attempted this route prior to Giotto, including Guglielmo whose crucifix in the Duomo at Sarzana depicts a Christ charged with passion and tension. Other works, such as those of Berlinghiero, Coppo di Marcovaldo and Guido di Siena, bear witness to the fervor with which art began to differentiate itself in terms of schools, influences and even political leanings. At Lucca, Romanesque painting is represented by the Berlinghiero family: the crucifix to be found in the gallery at Villa Guinigi is the only authenticated work of the father and shows, alongside certain Byzantine traces, a depth of expression that was already recognizably western. At Pistoia, Coppo di Marcovaldo—who many art historians recognize as the master of Cimabue—left a grandiose crucifix conserved in the Duomo. At Florence, it was to be Cimabue who determined the direction painting was to take, while at Siena the leading figure was Duccio di Buoninsegna. This also resulted in the dualism between Florence and Siena that was to dominate Tuscan art of the 14th century. In

119 On the right-hand side of the nave of the Collegiata (in the photo below, the interior of the church) there is a cycle of frescoes by Barna da Siena illustrating New Testament themes. From the founding of the church in the 13th century many artists contributed to its decoration: Taddeo di Bartolo, Benozzo Gozzoli, Bartolo di Fredi, as well as Domenico Ghirlandaio.

120 The two Sienese Maestà, *the one by Simone Martini (top) in the Palazzo Pubblico, and that by Duccio di Buoninsegna (bottom), now in the Museo dell'Opera Metropolitana, were painted within a few years of each other but show significant differences. Similar in compositional structure, identical in terms of subject matter, one is an affirmation of certainty, the other of doubt. One is still in the Byzantine tradition, the other displays Gothic trends.*

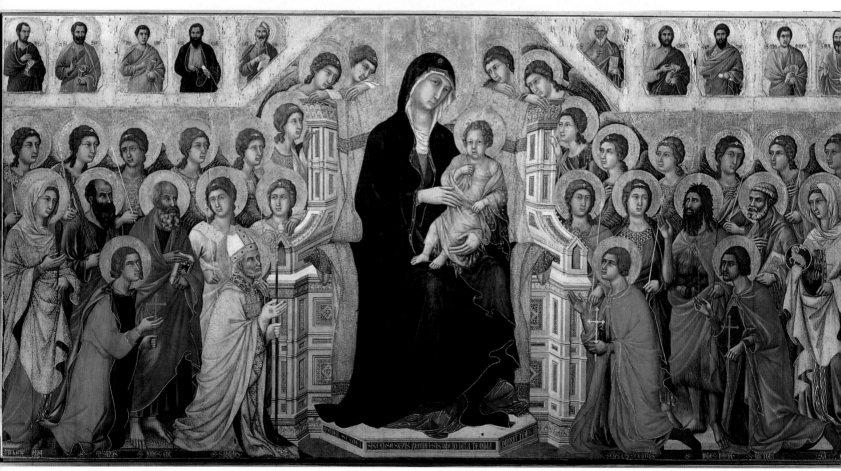

1308 the building committee of the Duomo of Siena commissioned Duccio di Buoninsegna to produce a great double-sided altar piece, the *Maestà della Madonna*. This was the work that marked Siena's definitive artistic break with Florence. As Giulio Carlo Argan was to write, "The result of the final consummation of Byzantine figuratism was, for Cimabue, a plastic condensation of the image and for Duccio a rigorously colorist anti-plastic condensation: beginning with these two, the history of painting was, in fact, to be the history of the relationship between form and color, between a plastic vision and a coloristic vision." Duccio's was a sophisticated, lyrical colorism, but one perhaps too cerebral to attract a significant following. The art of Siena was the result of a composite, open and evolved society, wealthy and proud of being so. The industriousness of the Sienese citizens was celebrated in the frescoes of the Sala della Pace in the Palazzo Pubblico: in his *Good Government* cycle Ambrogio Lorenzetti represented a life in which duty and pleasure were integrated, while in the Sala del Mappamondo Simone Martini celebrated the heraldic heroism of Guidoriccio da Fogliano riding his charger from town to town. He also tried to emulate the magic of Duccio's *Maestà*, creating an ideal of grace and vibrant beauty, of an almost courtly taste, and with a spatiality that had yet to be defined. The magnificent rise of Sienese painting was, however, destined to be short-lived, as with the death of its great masters that aristocratic sophistication was replaced with

art of a more concrete kind. Giotto was the undisputed protagonist of painting in the 14th century, a century also marked by the flourishing of so-called "vulgar" or vernacular literature. The artists and writers of the time were well aware of their Latin roots and rather than deny them they preferred to revive their ancient splendors, adding a new and fundamental element, that of nature. The intellectual aspect of Giotto's work—and this is in sharp contrast with the legend of the poor shepherd unaware of his own talent—led him to take an interest in other art forms such as architecture. He led a large workshop in Florence in which he worked with the pupils and disciples with whom he completed the frescoes of the Peruzzi and Bardi chapels in the church of Santa Croce. Toward the end of his career Giotto was appointed to the post of supervisor of building at the Duomo in Florence and in 1334 he began work on the Campanile of Santa Maria del Fiore: a three-dimensional interpretation of that clarity and purity that characterized his painting. Unfortunately, Giotto only survived to see the lower section of the tower completed. The work was eventually finished by Andrea Pisano and Francesco Talenti but without the crown planned by the maestro. Nevertheless, in spite of the alterations, the campanile is an important symbol, one of harmony and proportion, of the universality of art, the cardinal principle of the Renaissance. The classical ascendants that determined the evolution of Tuscan art also accompanied it through the late Gothic period. In Florence the renovation took place in a

121 The Madonna *of Ognissanti, now to be found in the Uffizi, fully illustrates the power of Giotto's art, with his revolutionary sense of space, color and composition. The intense humanity of the Virgin and Child dominates, with the slim structure of the throne of secondary importance.*

122-123 An object of veneration and also the target of vandals; the tomb of Ilaria del Carretto in the cathedral of San Martino in Lucca is probably the most celebrated work of Jacopo della Quercia.

The young woman was the wife of Paolo Guinigi, a nobleman of the city, and the memorial succeeds in rendering justice to her beauty in the candid white marble of the neighboring Apuan Mountains.

123 The themes of the castings composing the Gates of Paradise, the second door to the north of the Baptistery in Florence, were dictated to Lorenzo Ghiberti by the humanist Leonardo Bruni, and represent episodes from the Old

Testament, from Adam and Eve to Solomon and the Queen of Sheba. Ghiberti was also responsible for the first door, winning a celebrated competition in which Jacopo della Quercia and Filippo Brunelleschi also took part.

well-defined political and social moment. An antithesis to the highly aesthetic, courtly taste, it favored a more concrete and, it might be said, bourgeois vision of existence. Still linked to the late Gothic, Lorenzo Ghiberti represents an expression of the transitory moment, and in the celebrated competition for the reliefs for the second pair of doors for the baptistery in Florence, he defeated in 1401 his direct rival Filippo Brunelleschi with an almost perfect composition in which pathos was, however, virtually absent. In Siena it was Jacopo della Quercia who closed the cycle. Here he left, among other works, the *Fonte Gaia*, an exaltation in candid marbles. The tomb of Ilaria del Carretto in the cathedral of San Martino at Lucca is bathed in the mystery of pure harmony. Jacopo created a sarcophagus with classical traces inserted in a composition already showing Renaissance trends, a memorial to beauty and the love of Paolo Guinigi for his tragically young wife. There are notable sculptures in almost all the churches in the countryside around Lucca: wooden Annunciations of great expressive strength such as those of Partigliano, the *Angel* by Capannori and the *San Bernardino* in Borgo a Mozzano that some critics have linked with the name of Donatello. This was the moment of three great figures who, in different fields, opened Tuscan art to the universe. Brunelleschi in architecture, Masaccio in painting and Donatello in sculpture, set out in new and original

124 *Santa Maria del Fiore, the Baptistery and Giotto's Tower, in Florence form one of the world's most famous architectural compositions; a scenario that summarizes in a relatively compact area much of the history of Western art. Arnolfo di Cambio, Brunelleschi, Giotto and Ghiberti are but a few of the great artists who contributed to the decoration of the buildings.*

directions that Leon Battista Alberti, scholar and architect, was to describe in his treatises dedicated to the three arts. Their new philosophy derived from the different terms in which the conception and realization of the work of art were established: where previously the contents and even the iconographical lexicon were pre-defined and certain, the artist now had to find and define them autonomously. "Art is a process of understanding, the aim of which is not so much an understanding of the object as an understanding of the human intellect, of the faculty of understanding," (Giulio Carlo Argan). This way an all-encompassing revolution that swept away all that had gone before and arose in contrast with late Gothic aestheticism. Brunelleschi mutated the very concept of space, changing it into an expression of collective secular or religious sentiments. This was a crucial moment in the secularization of an art that continued to measure itself against the divine, but also, and above all, the human, against its history and its future. The cupola of Santa Maria del Fiore in Florence, erected without scaffolding, amazed contemporaries for its audacity and technical perfection, but above all for the totally new conception of space that it preached. The Spedale degli Innocenti was also born out of an interest in town planning, and works such as the church of San Lorenzo, and the Pazzi chapel, Santo Spirito, display a fascination with the plastic potential of forms, planes and arches. Similar sentiments fueled the work of Masaccio: the space that he constructed, austere and solemn, yet intensely human and geo-

metric, was real and concrete. The miracles, the Bible and stories and the evangelical events that he depicted were all subordinated to the concept of man, the narrative being rooted in history, with no concession being made to poetics. The frescoes in the Brancacci Chapel in the Church of the Carmine, the *Trinity* in Santa Maria Novella ("We may well imagine the surprise of the Florentines when, with the veil removed, this picture was revealed that appeared to have punched a hole through the wall to show a new chapel on the other side, built according to the modern style of Brunelleschi," Gombrich), the *Madonna* and the *Santa Anna* in the Uffizi have the strength of true, ancient and modern forms with no half measures. Donatello introduced another fundamental element to art: freed of its enslavement to architecture, sculpture became a harmonious blending of lines and planes, with a degree of popular and dramatic sentiment. His wooden crucifix (in Santa Croce), accused by Brunelleschi of being a "peasant," is the exemplification of an extreme realism that fears not the slightest hint of physical unpleasantness. Donatello portrayed the men of his time, from the *David* in the Bargello to the characters in the reliefs on the baptistery font at Siena, with almost violent gestures, a far cry from the prettified and static narration of Gothic art. The three artist-symbols were, of course, not the only figures to feel that something was changing in the field of art. Following on from the genius of Ghiberti and Donatello, it would be stretching a point to define Luca della Robbia

125 Dedicated to San Giovanni Battista, the patron saint of Florence, the Baptistery, mentioned by Dante, is a splendid example of Romanesque architecture. It is finished in green-and-white marble. The interior is illuminated by the mullioned windows as well as the lantern. The cupola itself is decorated with mosaics designed by Jacopo Francescano and executed by Venetian and Florentine artists, probably including Cimabue. The dominant figure is that of Christ presiding over the final judgment.

125

126 The David *by Donatello that can be admired in the Bargello in Florence. Donatello combined the classical ideals of beauty and harmony with an understanding of a new and modern civilization.*

as an innovator, but he does deserve a place in the history of art for his invention of vitrified terra-cotta, a decorative medium that immediately obtained great success and was to become a typical product of the Florentine craftsmen, with which he executed works that combined decorative, devotional and plastic qualities, such as the choir in Santa Maria del Fiore. Giovanni da Fiesole, also known as Fra Angelico, apparently more interested in the manifestation of the divine than the new man, captured the extraordinary power of Masaccio's spatial structure. His religious vocation did not lead him to reject perspective framework, but rather he incorporated it, as can be seen in the frescoes at the San Marco convent in Florence. The great Florentine artistic movements filtered through slowly to Siena as if smothered by an obstinate traditionalism: for Sassetta and Giovanni di Paolo art was not concerned with problems of understanding or morals. Another interpreter of Masaccio's themes was Filippo Lippi, a Carmine monk and therefore in close contact with the work of the master. Paolo Uccello, with the Creation scenes in the Chiostro of Santa Maria Novella in Florence, and above all the fresco memorial to Giovanni Acuto (Sir John Hawkwood) in Santa Maria del Fiore, tackled art from yet another point of view, that of absolute rigor in which passion was excluded in the name of coherent perspective. The few surviving works by Domenico Veneziano led to a synthesis of the defined space of Brunelleschi and Masaccio with the introduction of complex structures dominated by human figures. His work ran parallel to that of Andrea del Castagno who, with the *Last Supper* at Santa Apollonia in Florence, placed the accent on an exal-

tation of the physical. However, the perfect synthesis of form, color and perspective was to be found in the work of Piero della Francesca with his solemn, timeless forms. A stranger to Florentine culture, in the works surviving at Arezzo and Borgo San Sepolcro, Piero demonstrates that he was the true pivot between Tuscan art and that of Europe. The *Legend of the True Cross* cycle in the church of San Francesco (Arezzo) represents the artist at the height of his powers when he had already completed work in Urbino, Ferrara, Rimini and his hometown of San Sepolcro: the legend loses its medieval connotations, goes beyond the storytelling role and takes on a fully Renaissance and concrete vision of the world. As Longhi wrote, "The world of Piero unfurls as bright as a colored banner wrapping itself in a calm, indifferent destiny."

We have rather neglected architecture, which after Brunelleschi—and after Leon Battista Alberti, who by the mid-15th century had traced an early synthesis of the Renaissance philosophy, placing the accent on the enthusiastic study of antiquity and noble proportions—explored forms that were perhaps less rigorous, but certainly more varied. The Villa Medicea at Poggio a Caiano that Giuliano da Sangallo designed for Lorenzo dei Medici united the simple "rusticity" of a house destined for leisure pursuits with the subtle sophistication of a classical tympanum. A fundamental name is that of Bernardo Rossellino, the only architect who succeeded in realizing, albeit only in part, the Utopian dream of an ideal city. Commissioned by Pope Pius Piccolomini II, the "Humanist Pope," Rossellini designed and reconstructed the center of the village of Corsignano in the Sienese countryside.

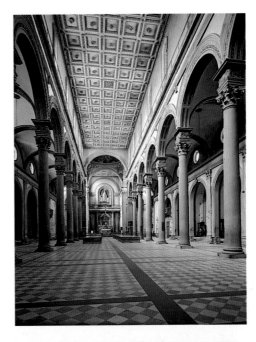

127 top left *Fra*
Angelico (the
illustration shows his
Deposition from the
Cross) *left much of*
his art in San Marco
at Florence. His
frescoes decorate the
choir, the Pilgrims'
Hospice and the
common rooms.

127 top right
Commissioned by
Cosimo I and
designed by Filippo
Brunelleschi
(Michelangelo
subsequently designed
a facade that was
never built), the
church of San Lorenzo
in Florence is a
triumph of the
Renaissance
architect's vision
and is articulated
with harmonious
spaces. The pulpits
by Donatello, with
panels narrating the
story of Christ's
Passion, are to be
found in the main
nave.

127 center
The Brancacci Chapel
in the Church of the
Carmine in Florence
is one of the greatest
Renaissance
monuments. The cycle
of frescoes begun by
Masolino da Panicale,
continued by Masaccio
and completed by
Filippino Lippi features
a wealth of significant
themes from the story of
Adam and Eve to that
of Saint Peter. In the
scene of Saint Peter
there is a self-portrait
of Masaccio, the painter
who perhaps best
represents the classical
and dramatic spirit
of Renaissance art.

127 bottom The
Legend of the Cross,
taken from the
Leggenda Aurea *by*
Jacopo da Varagine is
the theme of the great
fresco cycle by Piero
della Francesca in the
church of San
Francesco in Arezzo.
The "revolution"
inaugurated by Piero
lies in his stylistic
invention, severe
perspective structure
and the attention he
paid to the customs of
his time, as in the
scene of the meeting of
Solomon and the
Queen of Sheba.

The resulting town was renamed Pienza. It featured a nucleus of coordinated buildings that were proportioned according to the demands of perspective and the town became a unique, perfect monument to the reason of mathematics and classicism. The second half of the 15th century was marked by the work of another two great masters, Antonio Pollaiolo and Sandro Botticelli. Research is the common thread between the two, although they obtained differing and frequently contrasting results. A painter and goldsmith taken under the wing of Lorenzo il Magnifico, Pollaiolo combined the sharpness of Donatello and the richness of Domenico Veneziano and was the earliest influence on Botticelli. It was the latter who was to take art from one century into the next, passing from allegorical works charged with neo-Platonism, such as *Primavera* and *The Birth of Venus*, to the last series of compositions which were loaded with tragedy, an archaic sense of religion and spirituality. We have now reached the 16th century, the era of Michelangelo, Raphael and Leonardo, but Botticelli preferred to turn back, refuting science, perspective and anatomy. Leonardo the painter began his career in the workshop of Verrocchio. His distant landscapes that form the backdrop to many works demonstrate his interest in nature and the relationship with humanity that was developed in his scientific work. A fundamental work in this sense is the unfinished *Annunciation* to be found in the Uffizi. It was Leonardo, in his few works, who brought the 15th century to a definitive close. He traveled far afield, to Milan and into France, and another of the greats, Michelangelo, was also to enjoy greater success in Rome, away from his homeland. An overview of art in the middle of the century was provided by Giorgio Vasari in his *Lives of the Artists*. He placed Michelangelo at the top of the pyramid, with those artists who, not being able to match him, preferred tiredly to imitate him, placed on the lower tiers. The young Michelangelo also enjoyed the patronage of Lorenzo, who introduced him into the neo-Platonist circle. His Florentine works, from the *David* to

129 A portrait of a lady by Antonio Pollaiolo conserved in the Uffizi galleries. A painter and sculptor, Pollaiolo started out as a goldsmith and all his works reveal a search for formal perfection, but also an interest in anatomy and limpid, luminous coloring.

the *Tondo Doni*, from the sacristy at San Lorenzo with the tombs of Lorenzo and Giuliano dei Medici to the Laurenziana Library, display a tortuous development with profound research into nature and the spirit. The departure of Leonardo, Raphael and Michelangelo from Florence in the first decade of the 16th century left a significant vacuum. Florence itself was beginning to show signs of decline and the art world reflected this as it began a slow elaboration of the themes established by the great masters. There was no lack of important names including Frà Bartolomeo and, above all, Andrea del Sarto, who after having worked in Rome made good use of the experience in Florence, especially in the grisailles in the cloister of the Annunziata. Pontormo, on the other hand, was a more obscure figure in Tuscan Mannerism, perhaps influenced by the works of Dürer that at that time had begun to circulate in Florence. Under the patronage of the Medici, he completed a series of mythological frescoes in the villa at Poggio a Caiano in which his taste for classical culture was combined with a taut, nervous line. Tuscan architecture, in the meantime, was going through another period of great splendor with Antonio da Sangallo the Elder, the brother of Giuliano— responsible for the church of San Biagio at Montepulciano—and his nephew Antonio da Sangallo the

Younger who worked, above all, in Rome. Giorgio Vasari designed the Uffizi building, inserted between the Palazzo Vecchio, the Loggia della Signoria and the banks of the Arno, and along with Bartolomeo Ammannati was the greatest of the Mannerist architects. Ammannati was commissioned to extend Brunelleschi's Palazzo Pitti and also to build the Santa Trinita Bridge, a masterpiece of functionalism and technology. Bernardo Buontalenti, on the other hand, was invested with the honor of drawing up a town plan for Livorno. The small medieval town was cast aside in favor of an "ideal" city with wide, straight roads, geometrical piazzas and a broader more open appearance. At Pisa, a number of town-planning projects (for example Piazza dei Cavalieri) restored a dignity to the city that had since the early 15th century been somewhat overshadowed artistically speaking. In the field of sculpture, Benvenuto Cellini closed a cycle with the exaltation of technique (incomparable the pages of his celebrated autobiography in which he relates the story of the casting of the *Perseus* of the Loggia dei Lanzi at Florence commissioned by Cosimo I). This was the end of the Renaissance: along with the Grand Duchy of Ferdinand I, in the early years of the 17th century came forms of rationalism of a distinctly modern tone. Florence, in spite of its decline, still produced flashes of genius such as the

130 Michelangelo's David *is currently to be found in the Galleria dell'Accademia, but a faithful copy continues to stand in Piazza della Signoria, alongside* the entrance to the Palazzo Vecchio. Transformed into plaster or plastic fake marble, it is also available in miniature form to tourists at all the city's souvenir stalls.

decorations of the Palazzo Pitti by Pietro da Cortona, but it was substantially cut out of the Baroque movement. In Livorno in the middle of the 19th century Leopold II worked on further extensions of the city beyond the Medici walls, with colossal projects that transformed the port, and built one of Italy's first railway stations, but these were town-planning projects designed to modernize the city. There was a long period of artistic provincialism that lasted until the mid-19th century when Florence saw the rise of the Macchiaioli movement with its post-Romantic interest in the more banal and less heroic aspects of daily life. Fattori, Signorini, Lega and Abbiati, with their domestic and military scenes, their landscapes and sketches, were among the last exponents of the Tuscan painting tradition. After them were a number of adherents to the Futurist movement.

In conclusion, a few words about one of the most significant architects of the 20th century, Giovanni Michelucci, the designer of the Santa Maria Novella railway station in Florence and the church of the Autostrada del Sole, examples of extreme compositional freedom that is at once both measured and in absolute harmony with its surroundings.

131 top left The Tondo Doni, *an early work by Michelangelo, in the Uffizi, has recently been restored after being damaged in the bloody terrorist attack that destroyed the Accademia dei Georgofili bordering the gallery.*

131 top right The Museo dell'Opera del Duomo contains an unfinished Pietà *by Michelangelo. The work depicts Christ in the arms of Joseph of Arithmea: it would appear that the latter figure is actually a self-portrait of the artist.*

131 bottom Begun by Giorgio Vasari on the orders of Cosimo I and continued by Buontalenti and Alfonso Parigi, the Palazzo degli Uffizi was, as the name suggests, designed to house the offices of the Florentine administrative and judicial authorities. Today it contains the State Archive and, above all, one of the world's most famous art collections, initiated by the Medici, extended by the House of Lorraine and eventually taken over by the Italian state.

136 The tall facade of San Michele in Foro, the Duomo of Lucca, is triumphantly capped *with two final loggias formed from twisted columns and marble relief sculpture. The composition is* *crowned by the great statue of the Archangel Michael to whom the cathedral is dedicated.*

INDEX

MUSEUMS AND ART COLLECTIONS